Pomegranate Seeds
An Anthology of Greek-American Poetry

Pomegranate Seeds
An Anthology of
Greek-American Poetry

Dean Kostos, Editor

Somerset Hall Press
Boston, Massachusetts

© Copyright 2008 Dean Kostos, Editor
Published by Somerset Hall Press
416 Commonwealth Avenue, Suite 612
Boston, Massachusetts 02215
www.somersethallpress.com

All Rights Reserved.

Cover Image: Sofia Kontogeorge Kostos
Cover Design: Jonathan Soard

ISBN 978-9774610-4-2 (0-9774610-4-1)

Library of Congress Cataloging-in-Publication Data

Pomegranate seeds: an anthology of Greek-American poetry / Dean Kostos, editor.
   p. cm.
ISBN 978-0-9774610-4-2
1. American poetry—Greek American authors. 2. Greek Americans—Poetry. I. Kostos, Dean.
PS591.G74P66 2007
811'.6080889073—dc22   2006102342

CONTENTS

Preface	17
Nicos Alexiou	25
The Poet of the Diaspora	26
Images	27
The Survivor	28
The Green Prince	29
The Sad Girl	30
Manya Coulentianos Bean	31
Monody	32
Le Mot Juste at the Philadelphia Museum of Art	36
The Analyst's Body Ego	38
Dorothea Bisbas	41
Wreath of Desire	42
Midnight Moves	43
Lili Bita	44
Iphigenia	45
Kouros	48
The Center of the World	50
The Transformation	52
Sevasti Boutos	53
Memories of Aegina	54
Sunset	55
Seasons	56

John Bradley   57
If You Were Born with the Name Xidas   58
Song of Icarus   59
Naked Asides: For Yannis Ritsos   60

Ioanna Carlsen   63
Road Trip   64
When Hermes Whispers   65
In the Middle of the Night   66
Stay Up with Me   67
Windshield Wipers   69

Neil Carpathios   71
Coins   72
The Kiss   74
For the Vessel Within the Vessel   75

Yiorgos Chouliaras   76
Theseus: Mythology of Consciousness   77
Defenseless City   78

Kyriaki S. Christodolou   81
Homeland   82

George A. Christopoulos   83
Mirologion from Kalamata   84

Constantine Contogenis   86
Ikaria   87
There Are No Ploughs on Ikaria   88
Those Moments   89
Ikaros   91

George Economou   94
Kassandra's Story   95
The Amorous Drift
    of the First Hoplite on the Right Wing   97

Day of Disembarkation   98
An Evening in Kingfisher   99

Eleni Fourtouni   102
Killing Time   103
That Woman Said No   107
Untitled   110

Emily Fragos   112
Spindlers   113
To Balanchine   114

Dan Georgakas   115
Greek Widows of America   116
The New Jersey—Penwell   117
Pinball Purgatorio   118
Siciliana of the Byzantine Eyes   119

Faye George   120
Kore   121
The Call   122
Fotini   123

Aris Georgiadis   124
Summertime   125
Astoria: Sestina   126

Veronica Golos   128
A Bell Buried Deep   129
Re-Turn   131
Hollyhock Love Song   132
Persephone of Demeter   133
Demeter to Persephone   134

M.J. Golias   135
The Olive Grove   136

Ghazal	137
Translucent Homelands	138

Stathis Gourgouris — 139
Poseidonians (*Fin de Siècle*) — 140
For Kórinna (6th c. BC) — 142
The Dream of Penelope Delta — 143
Diver in Love with Oblivion — 144

Thea Halo — 145
Night — 146
Gift of the Gods — 148

Nicholas Johnson — 149
Back Home — 150
Point of Honor — 151
Smoking Villanelle — 152
Poor Company — 153

George Kalamaras — 154
In the Café of Strange Skin — 155
Banaras Is Another Name for the World — 156
Parthenogenesis — 158
On the Death of Miltos Sahtouris — 159
Looking for My Grandfather with Odysseas Elytis — 161

Nina Karacosta — 163
Dream — 164
Nostos — 165
Solitaire — 166

Penelope Karageorge — 167
Avenue "B" Rembetiko — 168
Exile — 169
Lipstick — 170
Lunching with Lola — 171
Prisoner of Summer — 173

E. D. Karampetsos   174
Waiting   175
Syntagma 1967   176
At the Reichenberger Griechenbeisl   177
The Last Months   178
Elvira's Lesson   179

Helen Dendrinou Kolias   180
Ιερή Ελιά   181
Pasta Flora   182
Barba Kostas   183

Sofia Kontogeorge Kostos   184
A Fortune Told   185
Litany of Tears   186

Dean Kostos   187
Introducing John L. Sullivan   188

Barbara Lekatsas   190
Hades   191
The Memory Tree   192
When I Was Small   193
Demeter in the Deep North   196

John Manesis   198
The Islander's Autopsy   199

Kathryn Maris   200
Goddess   201
Hansel in the Cage   202
Ophthalmology at Dawn   203
The End of Envy   205
The Boatman   206

Thanasis Maskaleris — 207
Sun Moon Lake — 208
Unnatural Tumbleweeds — 209

Andriana Mastor — 210
Greek Lessons — 211
To Love — 213
Hopper: *Rooms for Tourists* — 214
Chert — 216
Slate — 217

Cleopatra Mathis — 218
Living Next Door to the Center for Cold Weather — 219
Flowers — 222
Cleopatra Theodos — 223
The Source — 225

Zaharati Morfesis — 226
The King — 227
Subterranean Skies — 229

Nikki Moustaki — 230
Night Plumber — 231
Writing Poems on Antidepressants — 232
How to Write a Poem After September 11th — 233
Pita Bread — 235
Self-Portrait with Flowers — 236

Kostas Myrsiades — 238
Odysseus and Penelope
    Secretly Plot Against the Suitors — 239
A Centaur Prepares
    an Emigrant for His Journey Abroad — 240
The Emigrant Sets Out for America — 241
The House in Vourliotes — 242

Stephanos Papadopoulos	243
An Inherited Memory of War	244
Mavraki	245
Valparaiso	247
A Night in Bellavista	249
Andriana Rizos	250
Ghazal of Agapi	251
Today	252
Popped Stitch	254
Helen Ruvelas	255
Family Portrait	256
You Hold Yourself Proud	257
Nicholas Samaras	258
Studio Apartment	259
September in Tharri	261
The Need for Priests	262
Approach	265
The Sound of My Voice Like a Foreign Language	266
Minas Savvas	267
The Cemetery in Kukuvaunes	268
The Only Certainty	269
Women at Fifty	270
Hilary Sideris	271
Doug Craig	272
Route Seven Riverlawn Addition	273
Sex	274
Geometry	275
Eleni Sikelianos	276
First Greek Poem	277
Footnote to the Lambs	278
Ikaria's Tidepools	279

Diana Stamatelatos-Theocharis   281
For Yiayia & Papou   282
For Federico Garcia Lorca, "He Died at Dawn"   283
Smoking Reality through Cuban Cigars in Key West   284

Tryfon Tolides   286
Address   287
I Told Myself   288
New Moon   289
Poem Written
    Standing and Looking out the Window   290

Deno Trakas   291
End of August 2005   292
The Smaller House   293
All God's Mail   295
Labor Day, Pen and Spade   297
Grandfather   298

Dedicated to the memory of Kimon Friar

The largest largess
Of her fruits—
A blazing pomegranate
Bleeding in open hands.
      —Konstantinos Lardas

PREFACE

In addition to its mythological associations, the pomegranate may be thought of as the fruit of contradictions. Its meat is not firm like that of an apple or pear, but composed of ruby granules. And even though they appear to be hard, upon biting into them one finds they are bursts of liquid encased in crimson skin.

Similarly, this collection of poems—while reflecting a community's ethos—contains diverse aesthetics. All the writers share a connection (no matter how tenuous or pronounced) to their Greek heritage and to their American one. Of course, definitions of what it is to be Greek, American, or Greek-American are as varied and contradictory as the work of these poets.

Some of the contributors are from Greece or Cyprus, but call the United States home. While these people work in an American milieu, speaking English by day, they write their poems in Greek. As a result, some of the work in this book is presented in translation.

Most of the poets were born in the United States. Some claim little connection to their Greek origins and yet that heritage, that landscape, that history draws them back. Some of the American-born writers consider themselves outsiders in the prevailing American culture or, as poets, feel alienated by popular literary trends. Other poets, born abroad, have ambivalent feelings toward their Greek ancestry. Even for writers who actively shun or distance themselves from their background(s), that very act of rejection is a form of engagement.

Although it may no longer be fashionable to use it, I am interested in the hyphen that traditionally linked *Greek* and *American* because of its value as a metaphor—a little bridge between two worlds, two identities. Do we traverse this hyphen, leading us to divide our time, like Persephone, between two worlds? Are we Greek in America and American in Greece? Instead of this either/or proposition, perhaps another option exists: the hybrid identity. After all, like Persephone, who ate pomegranate seeds in Hades, we have partaken of both cultures, and have grown roots in both terrains. These roots have entwined with the words we write.

Nonetheless, many contributors felt the need to distinguish their Greek poems from their American ones. Most telling was the question poets commonly asked me: *do the poems have to be Greek in theme?* My answer was that they certainly could, but needn't be. Most contributors chose to send some poems that are Greek in theme, and others that aren't, representing their bifurcated selves. I found a number of the Greek-themed poems more engaging than the poems written on other topics, as if the writers had allowed themselves to dig more deeply with their pens (to paraphrase Seamus Heaney).

This brings to mind that the god Hades is also called Pluto, a name ultimately derived from the Greek word πλούτος, meaning "wealth." Indeed, precious metals are found beneath the earth's surface, and Pluto himself was rich in the souls of the dead. Like him, the writer's task is to go into the darkness—the uncharted and even unsettling realms that yield creative riches. By taking the risks necessary to explore the subterranean world of the psyche, one becomes a better writer.

In compiling this anthology, I see myself as a cartographer, attempting to map out a new terrain—a broader, more complex definition of what it means to be Greek-American. This requires challenging our assumptions and those that others may have about Greek culture, which tends to be associated with antiquity. Nobel-laureate George Seferis addresses this dilemma in *Mythistorema*, "I woke with this marble head in my hands; / it exhausts my elbows and I don't know where to put it / down" (lines 1-3). Aghast, the poet later reveals: "My hands disappear and come toward me / mutilated" (9-10. Translated by Edmund Keeley and Philip Sherrard).

So here is another pair of antitheses we involuntarily feel the need to bridge: the ancient Greek (which is revered) and the contemporary Greek (which is not). I'm not suggesting that we divorce ourselves from history. That's impossible, as Seferis implies. Even if we could eschew our connections to the Greek past, it would injure and diminish our writing. Besides, while countless writers—from Ovid on—have been inspired by ancient Greek myths, they can resonate more profoundly for a writer whose traditions and language provide a living conduit to antiquity. This recalls what Franco Zeffirelli said of Maria Callas—a Greek-American who portrayed a number of characters from ancient Greek literature—that she brought something extra to them. She created something new by fusing her Greek past with her knowledge of the Italian bel canto tradition.

We too are inspired not only by our ancient heritage, but also by its subsequent manifestations, when Greek culture commingled with others. The Hellenistic period dovetailed into the Roman period, setting the stage for Byzantium, which incorporated elements of both worlds. The Byzantine Empire itself was one of the longest in duration (over a millennium) and wide-ranging in its influences on both Europe and the Middle East, as illustrated by the Metropolitan Museum of Art's exhibition *The Glory of Byzantium* and in Colin Wells's book *Sailing from Byzantium: How a Lost Empire Shaped the World*.

The periods of Venetian domination yielded literary riches, such as the *Erotokritos*, as did the darker period of Ottoman occupation. After Greece's liberation, debate over the language issue, like sand in the proverbial oyster, produced a necklace of literary pearls: the luminaries of modern Greek poetry.

One of my reasons for referring to these various periods is to point out the resiliency of the Greek character. Even here in the United States, Greeks, while blending with the broader American culture, still retain their identity. As Kimon Friar wrote in the introduction to his seminal anthology *Modern*

Greek Poetry, "I know of no other country, at least in the Western Hemisphere, which has retained such identity and integrity under such crushing odds."

Political strife, wars, and poverty led Greeks and Greek-Cypriots to flock to America. Despite our many successes here, which we should celebrate, Greeks also suffered bigotry, hate crimes, and church burnings at the hands of the KKK and others. In response, the Greek organization AHEPA united with the NAACP and B'nai B'rith to combat discrimination. Greek-Americans also joined Archbishop Iakovos in supporting Dr. Martin Luther King, Jr. and the Civil Rights movement. In fact, on February 23, 1995, at an ecumenical commemoration honoring Iakovos, Coretta Scott King affirmed:

> At a time when many of the nation's most prominent clergymen were silent about the need to challenge racial injustice, Archbishop Iakovos courageously marched alongside Martin Luther King, Jr. Like many clergymen, Archbishop Iakovos could have avoided taking a position or he could have played a quietly supportive role. But Archbishop Iakovos heard a different drummer and decided that his religious calling required him to take a strong stand for justice and equality.

While the trials and triumphs of Greek-America have been memorialized in prose by gifted writers such as Gage, Papanikolas, Petrakis, Kallas, and Eugenides, this history still remains a fertile topic for exploration.

All the above-mentioned periods demonstrate some degree of cross-fertilization with other cultures; indeed, multiculturalism is nothing new. The ancient Greeks eagerly absorbed and reinterpreted Egyptian and Middle-Eastern influences (Ishtar becoming Aphrodite, for example). In this regard, Cavafy's project is instructive: his Alexandrian world teems with ghosts—Greek (pagan and Christian), Roman, Byzantine, Jewish, Egyptian, Islamic. By incorporating them and giving them voice, he enlarged our poetic capacity, creating something at once ancient and new.

But how do we adapt his legacy in the early twenty-first century? After all, modernism's injunction to *make it new* may have taken on another significance now that no "ism" predominates. This lack of one reigning aesthetic offers writers an exciting breadth of possibilities. Not unlike Cavafy, who forged a novel idiom by incorporating the full range of the modern Greek language—from *katharevousa* to *dimotiki*—we derive inspiration from a broader cultural spectrum.

We nurture our metaphorical and metaphysical imaginations with the diverse cultures that we encounter in our cities and those we experience in our travels, through the Internet, films, television, and reading. Latin-American literature and Eastern religions are two such influences. In this information age, we are exposed to a virtual onslaught of ideas and the latest literary theories from America, England, Greece, and elsewhere. Obviously many of the poets in this anthology read from wide-ranging sources, and are committed to a lively discourse on various trends and modes.

For that reason, I have assiduously avoided embracing any style over another. And yet I found one quality that pervades many of the poems in this anthology—surreality. For some poets, it's a mere undercurrent; for others, it's the primary aesthetic. If one believes in racial memory, then there may be an explanation for this phenomenon. Let's say that Greek mythology represents a kind of ur-surrealism. Therefore, perhaps on an unconscious level, myth's metaphorical archetypes and dark, irrational forces still inform our writing. I proffer this as one possible answer to a question that deserves further investigation.

When I mentioned this project to writer-fiends, they asked, "Are there *that* many Greek-American poets?" The response was a resounding "Certainly," yet I confess my surprise at how many gifted poets submitted work from every region of the United States. Some have published numerous books and won major awards; others have never been published before. This leads me to wonder: why aren't more of these poets known to a wider reading public?

Surely a listening audience exists, as evidenced by the considerable turnout every third Saturday at the Greek-American Writers' Association series, which I founded and have hosted since 1991 at the Cornelia Street Café, in Greenwich Village. My efforts there have been generously sustained by John and Judith Kallas, Penelope Karageorge, Barbara Lekatsas, Lili Bita, and Robert Zaller.

As thrilling as it has been to hear the sonic qualities of literature brought to life by human voices, readings dissolve into air; they're ephemeral. And so, as seeds grow into plants, my initial desire to provide a venue for voices that might otherwise have gone unheard developed into something larger. It was time to cull the talents of those I had been listening to (along with those of writers I knew only from afar) into the more enduring form of an anthology—the first of its kind.

As many seeds make up a pomegranate, so do these voices coexist in the following pages—separate, but whole. The person who brings this dream into the realm of reality is publisher Dean Papademetriou—the other Dean on this project. When I approached him with the idea over dinner at the Cornelia Street Café, he said, "Yes," with alacrity. That one word, like a shimmering seed, grew into this remarkable gathering of poems.

—Dean Kostos, Editor

POMEGRANATE SEEDS

NICOS ALEXIOU

Nicos Alexiou was born in 1959 in Volos, Greece. He studied Economics in Athens, while working at various jobs. He moved to New York in the 1980s and studied Sociology. Currently, he teaches Sociology and issues concerning the Greek-American community at the City University of New York. For years he has hosted and produced art programs for Hellenic public radio. Periodically he also contributes articles to the Greek and Greek-American press.

He has published three books of poetry: *Descent or The Specter of the Other Night* (1989) and *The Hidden Seal* (1996). His third most recent publication, *The Garden of Lost Vespers* (2006), includes new poems ("Wing of Clay") and completes a trilogy. Many of his poems, along with articles he has written, have been published in Greek and American journals and magazines.

THE POET OF THE DIASPORA

for Ioanna K. and Pantelis B.
The boundaries of my tongue are the boundaries of the world.

A man is counting sky-blue boats
in his blind palms
they tear open his hands
he travels on red seas

—The endless world is growing irreversibly smaller.

The woman's white hands like the flower
they once were
lift a petrified photograph
in which death smiles

—Whatever we loved is lost.

And he
with some broken words for wings
gestures to them awkwardly from behind
the evening enigma of language.

translated by Karen Emmerich, from *Wing of Clay*

IMAGES

The Sun
hurrying dead in a black hat
is nailing birds
to a perforated sky.

The Wind
hungry beast with iron teeth
howling shatters
the wings of the stars.

The Rain
blind old woman with rodents in her apron
mercilessly exterminates whatever accompanied the shadow behind
the wall.

The Sun. The Wind. The Rain.
Denial. Fear. And the Scream.

translated by Dean Kostos and Sofia Alexiou, from *Descent or The Specter of the Other Night*; previously from *Talisman*

THE SURVIVOR

In the central room of the morgue
after every battle
I wait for the trains of the conquered
the conquerors
the conquered.

As if this were the last time
as if nothing had ever happened, I ask
probable murderers
the date of death.

—My dear sir, they say, it's all right.
—Don't worry. Your corpse
is recognizable.
—Have a little patience.
—You will die.
—You will die.

translated by Karen Emmerich, from *The Hidden Seal*

THE GREEN PRINCE

For the past thirty-three years
since my death
a green prince
has been living in my mind.

Every day
he busies himself with the waters
the stones the fire.

Every night,
transforms into a piano.
Waits
for his beloved to come
and touch the keys
not with fingers, but her lips.

Only then
unfolds like a rosy dawn
a melody with no end
that hides unsuspectingly
in the conspiracies of the dark.

Solitude and the iris
have something in common:
hues.

translated by Dean Kostos and Sofia Alexiou, from *The Hidden Seal*; previously from *Talisman*

THE SAD GIRL

This woman
has in her heart
a deep wound

When the wound bleeds
she has in her heart
a silver moon

When the moon cries
she has in her heart
a little girl

who's afraid of the black dove

translated by Karen Emmerich, from *Wing of Clay*

MANYA COULENTIANOS BEAN

Manya Coulentianos Bean was born in Athens, Greece. She studied English Literature at the University of Athens. She then came to the United States, earned a Master's degree in Comparative Literature and continued with further graduate studies. She married and raised three children, while teaching people from many walks of life and a variety of ages from pre-schoolers to seniors. She worked for a time, for the New Jersey Council on the Arts as a resident poet.

Later, she studied psychoanalysis and is now a psychoanalyst in private practice in Philadelphia and New Jersey. Bean is a training and supervising analyst and faculty member at the Philadelphia School of Psychoanalysis and the Southern New Jersey Psychoanalytic Institute. In addition, she is a writer, educator, poet, translator, and grandmother of five. She has published extensively in professional, as well as in poetry journals and anthologies. Her book of poetry is entitled *Too Shy to Surrender*. She lives in Absecon, New Jersey.

MONODY

I

DURING THE HUNGER

In Athens, '42
        my mother brought the hen
next to her bed each dawn
        dozed with her finger stuck
in its behind
        she'd feel the egg
when it came
        saving it for me
before the hen
        could break it
and eat it herself.

II

BECAUSE I WAS THE YOUNGEST

I was the one
        to answer the door
when the beggar woman
        rang the bell
holding a sorry baby in one arm
        shoving
a tin cup in my face
        whining:
"Little lady, two drops
        of oil ... oil
may you grow
        into marriage

live
        in a big house
bigger than this
        one drop
please, child."
        The scream
of "Go away!"
        inside my head
the furious words
        lodged in my throat
of "Fool,
        fool of a beggar woman
talking
        your crazy talk
my mother
        if she had oil
she'd feed it to me"
        never came out.
Instead, I would just feel
        my eyes grow large
with staring
        then I'd remember
to shake my head "No."

III

THEATER

The little balcony upstairs
        with wooden shutters folded back
was a good place for me
        to watch the active world unfold
below, children my age
        would cease their playing to root
in garbage eating some orange peels
        and stuff I couldn't see or name

I'd watch in disgust
        then pity and shame
ashamed of hunger, stricken.

IV

BREAD STORY

If I walked the narrow streets
        around my neighborhood
and if I saw a person
        lying dead on the cement
such as the man with knees drawn up
        head resting on an empty plate
a tin cup by his side
        near his hands
if I felt hunger
        the fear of hunger
or hunger's consequence
        I'd think about our linen closet
how on top of clean folded sheets
        lay rationed bread
a piece for each one of us
        and how I could always sneak
and gather crumbs
        or even steal a tiny piece
from one fat slice
        and put it inside my mouth
and chew and slowly chew
        and then swallow.

V

WHITE BREAD

As an open German truck
      loaded with bread
drove downtown in Athens '42
      a thin boy jumped in
kept throwing loaves
      out to hungry people
like you might now throw gardenias
      to good musicians
until the driver stopped the truck
      and grabbing the boy's arm
with both his hands
      slammed across his knee—
broke it.

from *Too Shy to Surrender*

LE MOT JUSTE AT THE PHILADELPHIA MUSEUM OF ART

> *...and because the only thing left
> in the world for me then was poetry.* —Miro

As the floes of winter
intone their deep rumble,
hum, chant of mantras
gathering speed and rhythm
melody then harmony
and break
into polyphonous cantos, songs
or meditations on running water,
the Philadelphian can hear
Miro whisper to Klee
through walls, through
semi-permeable membranes,
the enigma of stone
washed smooth by the sea.

Gazing on the ladder
that reaches the firmament
she reflects on balance, gravity,
weight and counterweight,
on the uses of adversity.
Later she'll invoke
the Saint of the Inner Light
"More than anything," she'll say
"I want to be compassionate.
I've been harsh for too long
but now everything I touch
shall be touched gently..."

She'll live on the museum steps,
drink, sleep, dream,
awaken to the Oracle of Delphi

next to her beautiful brother,
as day by day Artemis
springs into her thought,
poised, her bow taut,
on the hunt for idea, word,
the right word, the timely action.

from *Too Shy to Surrender*

THE ANALYST'S BODY EGO
for Sidney I. Love

I

I am a dark and liberating statue
       my body a blue guitar
so send me your poor ex-
       patriates for salves
band-aids of Cyprian linen
       bring me your poem, the dream
the small disowned child
       split off and mocked
that yearns for legitimacy, its birth-
       right of smiling esteem.
Bring in the father fragments, yin,
       brother's hair, stones, earth
from home and the home-
       sickness and see if
our four hands and twenty fingers
       can fashion a new artifact
whole thing of soft tissue, yang,
       bone, water, and blood
a crazy potato head
       a new myth of the moon.

II

Swing low, you jazzmen
       bring me your freight train blues,
reggae, your syncopated
       dei-o bananas, play me
the spoons, tin pans
         "The Woman Is a Drum"

it's you and me tonight
        cool on the vibes
go to it, oh jazzmen, bang
        on the tambourine, moan
softly "like you wanted somebody terrible"
        alto saxophonists sound
the sound of ghetto
        child beaten in the sixties
Malcolm X, King.

Sweet chariot
        swing low, come
all your refugees and orphans
        bring me your un-, your dys-, and non-
your antisong, preverbal prattle
        your bubbling rage
your spit-and-shit
        let spit-and-shit cacophony
enter and resonate
        inside my hollow body.

III

And you Sidney-I-Love
        Ignatius and pugnacious
forever rubbing together
        your two wood legs
energetic, persistent cricket
        of Emotional Ed.,
start a bonfire
        and let's throw in logs
of defenses, sticks
        of resistances, large branches
of monumental original guilt

   the dead wood
of intellectualization
    tree trunks of massive
denial that are petrified
    and those scarecrows
of despair, frostbitten, dressed
    in misgivings and timidity
stuffed with regrets
    reluctance, with wrong reasons.

Let them burn
   all the way to Tierra del Fuego
and out the other side, Sid,
   like roses growing out of a foxhole
like hibiscus in a Greek August
   like red engines clanging and flashing
like things blazing
   and I, with spiked tiara now
falling off my forehead
   my brain a chainsaw on the loose
will join this Festival of Fires
   my tongue a flame that licks
spits, kisses and cleans.

from *Philadelphia Poets*

DOROTHEA BISBAS

Dorothea Bisbas was born and educated in New Jersey, where she lived with her parents and grandparents, all of whom are full-blooded Greeks. She is fluent in the language, as well as English and Spanish. After marrying, she moved with her husband to New Hampshire, where he practiced oral surgery. They came to California in 1961. She has three children and five grandchildren. She was widowed in 1986.

A lifelong proponent of poetry as a performing art, she has staged and participated in many readings. For the past nine years, she has conducted a weekly poetry workshop for the Rancho Mirage Library and with grants from The Friends of the Rancho Mirage Library, has produced seven anthologies of the works from her group, which meets year round.

Her own book, a lyric epic on the life of her immigrant grandmother, was published in 2002. The poem "Wreath of Desire," which follows, is the title poem from that book. Residing in Palm Desert, California, she is currently collecting her poems for another volume.

WREATH OF DESIRE

This Sunday, silence cools the air.
Nearby, the aromatic incense
smokes through the church doors.
The villagers have gone to pray.

Alone, here at a doorway,
its blue paint flaking beneath
a wreath of lilacs
dried from another season,
a tiny key clings to a rusty nail.

I covet that key,
I want to enter the door,
throw open the dusty shutters,
wave a lacy handkerchief
at all the passersby
calling them by name
as if I'd always lived there

as if that bed with its tattered quilt,
that spindly chair
those tintographs on the flowered wall
were mine
and I'd been born in that room.
I want to live that life,
the Greek life
for a little while.

MIDNIGHT MOVES

We wait for the pulse to throb
late parties in the taverns by the sea
serving food mostly about salt
tiny rings of calamari
olives shiny and black
as the eyes of Greek women
eggplant smothered in garlic
snow-white cubes of goats' milk

euphoria comes in ouzo on ice
sip after cloudy sip
now the music starts
a wild-eyed bouzouki player
strumming his heartstrings
a clarinetist wailing licorice notes
that wind into the smoky air
guitars amplify our heartbeats
as we tap our feet
to the pain and love

three men circle their shoulders
their feet finding precision so perfect
they are one body
we join them
a circle of shoes tapping to the music

someone throws a plate
it cracks into a hundred chips
we dance around the wasteful tribute
celebrating being alive
being joyfully exuberant
being Greek

LILI BITA

Lili Bita was born on Zakynthos. She received degrees from the Athens School of Drama and the Greek Conservatory of Music before immigrating to the United States, and has performed classical and modern drama as well as her own one-woman shows on three continents. She is the author of ten books of poetry, most recently *Lightning in the Flesh: New and Selected Poems* (Iolkos, 2003), two collections of short fiction, a novella, several plays, and a memoir, *Sister of Darkness* (Somerset Hall Press, 2005). In addition, she has translated Anaïs Nin's *A Spy in the House of Love*, Joy Stocke's *In the Cave of the Bear*, and, with Robert Zaller, *Thirty Years in the Rain: The Selected Poetry of Nikiforos Vrettakos* (Somerset Hall Press, 2005). Her work has been translated into several languages, has received a number of awards, and has been widely anthologized. She lives in Bala Cynwyd, Pennsylvania.

IPHIGENIA

I

Didn't you call me
your little girl,
propping your legs
on the gilt desk
for me to climb on,
you the horse
and I the rider?
Wasn't it you
who let me scrawl
across the golden page
of the Mycenaen laws
because you enjoyed seeing
the strange oracles
of my childish finger?

Wasn't it you
who, when on full-mooned nights
I climbed from tree to tree
and stone to stone
in the sinister gardens of the palace
and the wind danced
without your leaves in my hair,
cast a burning look
on my nascent puberty
with grief in your gaze
to think it must some day belong
to one of your generals?

Later I saw you
come through the palace gate
locked in bronze armor

your soldiers greeting you
with a battle cry
and my mother, Clytemnestra,
holding me in the embrasure
of the window,
her arms stretched toward you
as if over the rim of a precipice,
the stones below sharp and dry.

You, Agamemnon, judge
of others' passions,
you never even turned
to look at your little girl,
mute with the ice of your betrayal.
From now on,
new words rule our lives
like circling panthers.
Helen. Paris. Troy.

II

My old nurse,
keeper of the household gods,
pulled at her white hair
when Agamemnon's messenger
brought a sealed letter,
crying,
Don't go to Aulis harbor,
the omens are dismal,
I saw the child in my dream
adorned like a bride
in a black shroud
instead of a wedding ring
the blade of a knife.
Send the messenger back
with the seal unbroken.
Don't go.

III

Aulis harbor,
Serene, a dead oyster.
The ships afloat
like the paper boats
we sailed on the palace lake.
The army cheered
when we entered the encampment,
the mules laden
with my wedding preparations,
but seeing me
cast their gaze to the ground.
My father turned his eyes away.
Let's do it quickly, he said,
while Clytemnestra tore open her robe
and pressed me close
as if she'd swallow me live
into the womb again.
We started running together,
crying, Murder.

The knife's blade
slices my neck
like the watermelons
my father cut with relish
at family dinners.
The wind stirs,
calling the army
to its ships.

Am I not your little girl,
Father, for whom you
propped your legs
on the ornamented desk
so that I could ride, ride your knees
and fall into your arms?

translated by Robert Zaller

KOUROS

Here, in this cradle, this grave
this scooped-out gully shorn of growth
the great body of the kouros lies.
Fruit trees bend over him
their heavy wealth.
The black-hooded horse
turns the yoke of the well
a clock that tells no time.
Falling apples
the dry cough of birds
the percussion of a waterfall
chime the toneless centuries.
His room is simple, unadorned
as befits a young man's gravity.
Roofless, so that his gaze
adjusts itself to the infinite,
the glitter and size of the abyssal night.

Unclasping your hand,
I climb the stone steps
to where the naked body
lies like a spent athlete
laureled with victory, avid
for still wilder triumph.

The leg is severed
at the knee.
I sink my fingers
deep into the cleft
feeling the hard fracture
of the marble
lovingly I sculpt
the perfect body

the massive stiff shoulders
the mound of the pectorals
the hard clump of sex
winnowing away the centuries
that separate us
pinching and caressing
sucking welts to the white surface
like buried fruit.

Dusk falls in the quarry.
The workers leave their tools,
belt their robes, and walk back to Naxos.
The kouros stays alone, unfinished,
and in the hovering dark
I come again
to bruise the chastity of stone
with the hunger of my human flesh.

translated by Robert Zaller

THE CENTER OF THE WORLD

Each day they come to the spring
anointing their hair with bay oil
to shame the sun
they close their doors behind them
lifting the empty jugs
like dancers their veils
they tread the dry earth,
fisted with clods, prickled with chaff.
The waves crash on the island's shore,
the north wind snakes through the trees,
teaching their song the laws of desire.
They let the water glide over them,
soaking the pastures hardened
by years of servitude
under the same plow.
Ah—for a moment then
in this sun-drunk solitude
the world belongs to them.

Far away,
a shepherd sings his lament
the women quiver
like dry lightning
consecrating themselves
to the pleasure-pyre of the sun.
The dogs bark them back
to their duty.
Sentinels line the path back home.
The women bend forward,
lifting the jugs to their heads,
filled for the tub and the sty.
A flock of birds stitch the sky
with black thread.

The door will close
on the woman, the man, the child,
and the crust of bread.
A drop of water softens it.
Tomorrow
the north wind will blow.

translated by Robert Zaller

THE TRANSFORMATION

We sit, arms linked
as if to a chain,
the dark sideboard
with its stained ornaments
looming behind us,
the dowry of the departed.
On the Christmas table
the empty dishes lie
like vacant faces,
the knife thrust in the loaf
it hadn't the strength to cut
and those three wine glasses,
I don't remember how many times filled,
stones lugged down the throat
to settle at the bottom
of our separate hells.
Tomorrow we'll show
our mutilated stumps at the airport
and shrink the world to a sob.
All ready? The photographer
lines us up in his sights
and we take our grinning places.
Hold it! Just like that!

They left me their smiles,
the dregs of the wine,
the knife still stuck in the bread.
Today was the day.
Winter rains strips the last leaf
and bury the last of the dead.
The photo sits on the sideboard
terrible as an ancient statue.

translated by Robert Zaller

SEVASTI BOUTOS

Sevasti Boutos was born and raised in Athens, Greece. She studied veterinary medicine in Greece and was trained for small animal surgery in England. She practiced in her own veterinary office in Melissia for eight and a half years. In 1988 she immigrated to the United States, where she studied pure and applied mathematics and graduated with honors. Since 1998, she has been employed as a computer lab coordinator at Barnard College of Columbia University.

Boutos is also a radio show producer and magazine and newspaper columnist. Her first poetry collection – *My Two Homelands* – circulated in May 2005. She has received the following awards for her poetry: Certificate for "One Greek Mother (Korinthos, November 2003); First Award for "My Two Countries (International Greek Writers, March 2004); Special Award for Culture and Peace for "Olympic Armistice" (Unesco, November 2004); Special Award for *My Two Homelands* (Xasteron, Greece); Special Award as the most distinguished Greek-American journalist (from the Mayor of Neo Psyhiko, Athens, Greece).

Boutos also established The Aristotle Award for work ethics and academic excellence. She presents this award annually at the Academic Technologies Department of Hunter College in New York.

MEMORIES OF AEGINA

I remember
the green apron the yard wore,
and the cicadas glued to the pistachio trees
loaded with seeds, singing "hurrah,"
muted by a flock of pigeons that blocked the sky
on their midday flight.

And when we were coming back from the sea,
covered in sand, I remember the fountain
rinsing the seaweed and dried mud
from our bodies, washing dishes
or watering the thirsty wayfarer,
blessing us with wishes.

That meal, *piyaz* for us, *turlu* for others,
squash with potatoes dipped in olive oil,
I remember throwing to the chickens
scared of my mother.

How to forget
the exuberant red tomatoes before harvest?
Drowsy hornets, sweetened from the August grapes,
stinging our lips and swelling them like apes?

But, mostly I remember my grandparents—
their memories,
a commemoration mass to others.

translated by Shterna Wircberg, from *My Two Homelands*

SUNSET

The last goodbye
I want to stammer to you.
In that sunset when time stoops,

I want to hear your voice
created from vespers,
bidding farewell.

I want to see the color of sunset
like a couple of pigeons,
broken—put them in a boat
with the rotating sun.

translated by Shterna Wircberg, from *My Two Homelands*

SEASONS

I like the blond summer sun
that reveals wrinkles
and the wind in winter rustling the body.
In the spring
the vibrant trees
cause the heart to grin like a shell.
Autumn makes me sad,
its melancholy
buried deep in the earth.

translated by Shterna Wircberg, from *My Two Homelands*

JOHN BRADLEY

John Bradley is the author of *Love-In-Idleness: The Poetry of Roberto Zingarello* (Word Works), *Terrestrial Music* (Curbstone), and *War on Words* (BlazeVOX). He has edited *Atomic Ghost: Poets Respond to the Nuclear Age* (Coffee House) and *Learning to Glow: A Nuclear Reader* (University of Arizona). He lives in DeKalb, Illinois, with his wife, Jana, and their cat, Luna. He teaches writing at Northern Illinois University. His Greek background reflects the perils of the immigrant assimilation success story. Allegedly fleeing Greece to avoid military service, his Greek grandfather, Michael Xidas, came to America at twelve and eventually settled in Charleston, South Carolina, where he ran a grocery store. He married a non-Greek, Theresa Thornley (ethnicity unknown, as she had been adopted as a child). They had four daughters—Mickey, Mary, Beverly, and Theresa—and endured an unhappy marriage. The author met his grandfather once as a young child, shortly before his grandfather's death to cancer, but sadly has no memory of him. After Xidas's death, confusion arose over his place of birth—the family thought it was Crete, but his death certificate states Chios. Bradley's mother, wanting to be seen as an "American," never learned Greek or had interest in Greek culture. The paternal side of Bradley's family is Irish, and was more interested in being assimilated than keeping alive its Irish culture. Bradley hopes one day to visit Greece.

IF YOU WERE BORN WITH THE NAME XIDAS

You want to bury it
inside a bag of owl hair,
says the moon.

You want your mouth
to lose control when a crow
wing brushes your own.

You want someone to kiss
your flesh in the one
way no one has ever bothered,
says the moon.

You want to let
a series of red threads
dangle from your live eyebrows.

You want to make a sound
like a piece of wood
making love to something
on the other side
of the wall,
says the moon.

How the moon
knows so much
about my mother's
maiden name
cannot be told.

SONG OF ICARUS

He was always warning me
about something or other.

"Groom your wings
or the winds will mock them."

"Fly too near the sun
and he'll clip your wings."

Rules, rules, rules.
I live in the absence
of rules. The space
beyond all rules.

My wings and I flew far above
the old man and his old man fears.
Until the sun began to melt

my song and I dropped through
a hole in the sky into the sea
where each afternoon at three
I drown all over again.

At least that's the story
the old man wants you
to believe.

Let him enjoy his grief.

I tell you I didn't die.
I just never bothered
to turn back.

NAKED ASIDES: FOR YANNIS RITSOS

Before you eat my bread
tell us a joke
about when you were
still a fool.

*

Sleeping on your tongue
all the music I need
to tell you what can't be
sewn into words.

*

How is it my poems
sound so much better
when you read them
in bed naked?

*

You repair a broken
cloud with bits
of cloud breakage.

*

Her body shrinks
and shrinks. Outside
on the roof, a star
skeleton smolders.

*

After long silence
I opened my mouth.
No one likes the taste
of snail blood.

*

That lump
on my finger—
where oblivion and I
exchanged addresses.

*

Our hairs gather and toss
on the fallen floor.
What god would not
stop and love them?

*

Your image in wood
my hand covets. Or
does the still tree
covet you more?

*

Just don't speak
my name aloud
when you embrace me
in Hades.

*

In the house of photographs
no one did I recognize
not even my own salt.

*

Taking the rain
apart, I piece
together your face.

*

Either way, he said,
we're all related
to the furthering night.

IOANNA CARLSEN

Ioanna Carlsen's parents came from the Peloponnesos (mother) and Andros (father) and somehow ended up in St. Louis. Later they moved across the river to Alton, Illinois, where she grew up; they always went back to St. Louis to go to one of the three Greek Orthodox churches there. Carlsen left Alton to attend the University of Illinois, where she received a BA in English, and an MA in Linguistics.

Her poems and stories have appeared in *Poetry, The Hudson Review, Nimrod, Poetry East, Café Solo, Chelsea, The Quarterly, Field, Apalachee Quarterly, The Marlboro Review, Columbia, Solo, Alaska Quarterly Review, Mondo Greco, Prairie Schooner, Quarterly West, The Gingko Tree Review, The Beloit Poetry Journal, Glimmer Train*, and many other literary magazines. Her poems have recently appeared in *Nimrod* and *The Cimmaron Review*; her work is forthcoming in *Agni*.

She was a featured poet for March 2001 online at *Poetry*. She was also featured online at *Poetry Daily* on April 9, 2001. One of her poems was chosen for Billy Collins's *Poetry 180*. She won the 2002 Glimmer Train Poetry Open.

She lives in Tesuque, outside Santa Fe, New Mexico, with her husband, Chris.

ROAD TRIP

I've always wanted to paint
the way the road eats up your life,
the way you drive right into it,

how at night the street signs, catching your lights,
take on the mood of the music on the radio, tilting sadly to the right—
how even during the morning the soft whir of the car
brings you so close to sleep
you can see the wheat in the fields
through your eyelids,

how in the late afternoon,
over small poolings of water reflecting trees against the sky,
birds fly through birds,
one flock through another—
wings almost touching wings
in spite of so much space around them—

how barns were called hip-roofed,
how words exist in time like anything else,
and fly through other words,
their wingtips brushing other wings,
how some sleep now
under the fields behind closed eyelids,

how tonight, after the substructure of the rural,
we look forward, toward
the hard edges of the city,

how it all passes
how all the things you dread
shall come to pass,
and also pass,

wings whirring by wings
and the idea of infinity.

WHEN HERMES WHISPERS

Oh good,
      you've had a lucky streak,

Hermes, who's saved you time and again,
is here for the last time—

the one who turned the feet of cattle backwards,
invented shoes that hide their own footsteps,

      that one—
who makes you invisible,
all the while a dog barking at your heels—

he guides you into the tent of Achilles,
gives you a last good meal,
saves the body of your oldest son,

then sees you off at dawn into the arms of luck,
      the beginning of all things.

IN THE MIDDLE OF THE NIGHT

A passing headlight enters
a rectangle of window,
fans the room, trailing
a long distance behind it;
kindles on the gold rim of a lamp,
then slips away.
Leaves you pacing
the outskirts of sensible sleep.

On the other side
of the window, the street.

Beyond it,
what you wanted most, yet feared,
revealed:
nothing really ending, something
always slinking forward,
stairs rising in the opposite grass,
and soon, birds waking,

throats and wings opening
like so many doors.

STAY UP WITH ME

Because I don't want to sleep,
stay up with me,

but if you do sleep
go back to where you were before,
it will be familiar.

If knowing is being in a past tense,
a present that is, *was*,
a present that *is* goes back.
Isn't that how I know what I know,
by having been what I was?

Relativity incarnate—
any day now
I'll explode into night
like a star.
Stay up with me,

that's how I'll know what I was—
seen by something, watched,

slipping between intervals of the visible,
a morning snagged in its shadows,
hooked on a breath,

fire coming from the east,
a premonition,
light branding the floor, call it sun—
spells, divination by shadow,
salt, dice, dreams, ink,

the dough of cakes, corpses,
stay up with me—
when the furniture burns,
even I know how brilliant
the idea behind everything is.

WINDSHIELD WIPERS

I

The bus uses up the road
from Boston to Amherst,
beating off an elemental rain
the dense foliage absorbs.
The sweep of the windshield wipers—
small waist, long arch of hem,
invisible dress wading across the wet glass—
lets you witness for a moment what you're getting into,
the intense greens of Massachusetts,
the sound of the wipers a metronome,
clearing the scribbled past,
and then creating a space in time,
a meter stepping into the same subject—

the world, not the world,
the world, not the world—

what it's like to be living,
fogging the windows with breath,
and what it will be like
coming back the other direction,
baptized in absence,
this wetness no obstacle,
this road no map.

II

The bigness of the arc going each way,
never deviating in its rhythm,
the back, the forth,
the pen writing its line
and then returning,
starting over again,
the world, not the world,

every swing across the glass
clearing you into the present,
into the pause
between the wedge that appears
where the wipers have just left,
and that recurring fog of absence,
their leaving,
where you are *not in the world—*

where the wipers
squeeze out of rain
a new thought the glass speaks:

come back, come back.

NEIL CARPATHIOS

Neil Carpathios is the son of two Greek parents—father from Athens and mother's family from Rhodes. He attended the Iowa Writers' Workshop and has since lived in Ohio. His poetry has appeared in numerous magazines and anthologies, and he is the author of several award-winning chapbooks. His first full collection, *Playground of Flesh*, was first runner-up in *Main Street Rag*'s book competition and was published in their poetry series in winter of 2006. His second collection, *At the Axis of Imponderables*, won the *Quercus Review* Poetry Series Annual Book Award; it was published in 2007. He is an associate poetry editor of *Artful Dodge* magazine, and a professor of Creative Writing at Walsh University. He also has taught high school English for the past eighteen years.

COINS

Here's the last stop
of a man who was buried
without shoes, feet
swollen from infection;
who taught me chess,
pretending to lose every game;
who showed me the transparent
model man, took out
plastic organs in his hand,
each a different color,
heart, liver, brain,
and explained their functions;
who fell off a mule
and broke his elbow,
still crooked; who worked
as a surgeon cutting out
tumors and made fancy
crosses from Popsicle sticks;
who sneaked his son early
from church to escape
dull sermons; who saw
every war movie made
and never grew a beard
but could have in a week;
who arrived in America
with twenty bucks
and a battered valise;
who was married to the same
woman thirty-nine years
and proposed on the first date
and had three children
and two grandkids he gave
rides on his horseback;

who with his son in Madrid,
sat drunk on sangria,
raw squid on plates
still full of black ink;
who died at seventy-one,
lungs full of water
and gave me the ring
his mother gave him
before coming to America,
Alexander the Great
carved in gold
I wear on my finger;
who always jingled coins
he gave the paperboy,
and kids at the bus stop;
who in the remotest corner
of this graveyard lies,
where even now,
my boots sinking in mud,
I can hear chinks
of silver in his pockets
rising up through the dirt.

from *College English*

THE KISS

By freezing passion at its blossoming
perhaps Rodin knew he challenged
Sophocles who said as lover you want
ice to be ice yet not melt
in your hands. How stone,
implying permanence, might let us believe,
a moment, the seated figures are beyond the leaf
that cannot keep from letting go the branch,
beyond even stupidly purpling grapes
that do not understand the process
by which they darken, darken nevertheless.

from *Poetry*

FOR THE VESSEL WITHIN THE VESSEL

They say Alexander on his deathbed wept.
Not because of pain or because
he was leaving behind the miracle
firmness of a woman's breast.
Not because he would never see
another sunrise, taste another succulent
pear. Not because he would never again
feel the sudden gush of blood on his hands
withdrawing the sword, the animal rush
that ensued. Not because of the tangle of stars
he explored sitting outside his tent
countless nights after war. Not because
of wine, watermelon, the sound of birds.
Not because of passion or the gradations of love.
Not even because of the music of thought,
deep resonance inside the jeweled crater
of the skull as he stood watching
wind barely graze the tops of trees,
the ocean speaking in waves.
He wept, they say, for the soundless ballroom
of the body, where spirits of those times
we're most alive dance. Where what lasts
by not lasting expands what we are,
cracking us. For what, they say, held it all,
he wept. And for what he could now hold.

from *The Carolina Quarterly*

YIORGOS CHOULIARAS

Yiorgos Chouliaras is the author of six volumes of poetry in Greek and numerous essays–in Greek and in English–on literature, cultural history, and international relations. Reviews and translations of his work have been published in leading periodicals, including *Agenda*, *Grand Street*, *Harvard Review*, *Modern Poetry in Translation*, *Poetry*, and *World Literature Today*. Born in Thessaloniki and educated at Anatolia College, Reed College, and The Graduate Faculty, New School for Social Research, he worked in New York as a lecturer, advisor to cultural institutions, correspondent, and press officer. He has served as Press Counselor at the Greek Embassy in Canada, in Athens during the Olympic Games, and Director of the Greek Press & Communication Office at the Greek Consulate in Boston. He is currently Director of the Press and Communication Office at the Greek Embassy in Washington, D.C. He was a founding editor of the influential Greek reviews *Tram* and *Hartis* and an editor of literary and scholarly periodicals in the United States. An Emeritus Member of the Board of the Ottawa International Writers Festival, he was elected and served on the Executive Board of the Hellenic Authors' Society as Vice President for international relations. His retrospective poetry volume in Greek, *Roads of Ink*, is available from greeceinprint.com in the United States. Several of his poems have been translated by David Mason—an award-winning poet, essayist, and translator.

THESEUS: MYTHOLOGY OF CONSCIOUSNESS

It is late now
and that may be why I can't remember

narrow passages follow rectilinear
galleries and endless corridors
indelible turns
blinding alleys in the dark
I walk without stopping, up and down steps
I move in circles repeating
my footsteps' rhythmical sounds

a thick odor follows me constantly
paces ahead of me
clings to me: everywhere with me
I've already been here
I know the place

And somewhere in its cold shiver
anxiety's small caterpillar is stirring
able at any moment to change itself
into the huge dark butterfly
overshadowing with its wings
the childhood hiding places of my life

It is impossible for me to remember
how this ball of yarn found itself in my hands
endlessly unraveling
once, twice, countless times
wherever I pass
always a step ahead of me
yet without guiding me
without showing me
what I'm doing here
and where I may find myself at the end

from *Agenda*, translated by David Mason and the author

DEFENSELESS CITY

My wife was not born in Missolonghi.

Later, she would go down alone to the water
perfectly smooth, waveless
ever ready to accept the sun
when it finally decided to soften
its colors upon the lagoon
shamelessly reddening the edges
of a horizon without perspective.

Where were they going, those who saved themselves
escaping to the embraces
of the girls from the city where
the crippled poet died, having brought
all that money for the revolution?

Late in the day, thousands of nights ago in London
as we took the dogs out for a walk
we realized that the historian would
have been much harder on the Greeks
or at least with us, had we not been his guests.
We paid dearly for Byron's money.

Those were the years of another revolution,
as they used to say in Greece, and the English
philhellene held accountable only
the descendants of those who were saved in the exodus.

I have also seen the salt from a distance
getting drier and thirstier
while the neighboring water so carelessly
flaunts its glaring wetness
to the dead poet's countrymen

while the sun sets ever so slowly
tracing the cenotaph of the empire.

At a reception in England, Don Juan,
for those who consider every poem autobiographical,
overheard or was told of a woman
who sternly warned her daughter:
Don't look at him. He is dangerous
when you look at him.

I live to make you happy
I didn't say to her, because, if it's impossible
I prefer you to be unhappy is what they'd say
those who like straight talk
and die talking to themselves
in little, everyday revolutions.

Marriage is a difficult story.
Marrying history is difficult.

Shelley's wife, Mary, bore
a monster of our own.

We are all Greeks, her husband used to tell her
just like I still hear from his countrywomen
who would prefer that I were English.

Solomos, without ever having taught
at an English school like Kalvos did,
decided not to become an Italian poet.
His mother's language a domestic servant
and in fragments survived
as if he were an ancient author.

Across the water, the two of them keeping company
in the Zakynthos square greet the tourists

taking a little plunge
into the murky waters of culture.

You would have to be there, she tells me
at the exodus festival of today—
three days and nights of drinking and
making rounds on horseback
from tavern to tavern while in front
the drums are played only by Gypsies.

Missolonghi was a city before the birth of Palamas
and Athens was a village
and the capital of the kingdom.
In days of democracy a former successor to the throne
gets married to a little princess
of an American dynasty and their kid
must dance as Greeks do,
just like Anthony Quinn.

A friend came to see us in New York where we live
not too far from the water.
We buy Greek salt.
We plan the exodus every year.

Translated by Peter Hasiakos with the assistance of the author, this poem was awarded the First Undergraduate Prize in the Contexts for Classics translation competition of the University of Michigan in 2006.

KYRIAKI CHRISTODOULOU

Kyriaki Christodoulou was born and raised on the island of Cyprus. In 1974 her homeland was invaded and, three decades later, it is still occupied by the Turkish armed forces. In October of the same year, she arrived in the United States in pursuit of higher academic studies. Her early attempts in poetry and prose in Greek, won her awards by the Pancyprian Literary Association in Cyprus (KLON).

She is a graduate of Hunter College of the City University of New York with a Master of Science Degree in Social Research. She is currently the Executive Director of the Cyprus Children's Fund a not-for-profit organization based in New York aiding needy children on the island of Cyprus. In 1995 she was awarded the Woman of the Year Award by the Pancyprian Association of America, in recognition of her services to the community.

She is a wife, mother, part-time educator, and gardener. She loves reading, writing, traveling and music and is currently working on a short story. She resides with her husband and son in Queens, New York.

HOMELAND

Tell me about your country.
Where did your people come from?
Need I revisit my heart,
my soul's threadbare fabric?
The old woman
I become that very moment.
Like Mother often says:
Way before your American life,
your American dream
beauty knew no bounds
in my country of infinite wisdom.
Legends and myths live on.
But it's true after all.
For I, too, know
of splendid exteriors
of lovely legends and myths
ghosts of lives past.
The spring-fragrant blossoms
now grace tombstones.
I know of those who left
of those who stayed behind.
As a matter of courtesy
before you I stand
into the liquid carbon of your eyes
I stare
wondering—you walk away—
who the millennium man will be.

GEORGE A. CHRISTOPOULOS

George A. Christopoulos, a native New Yorker who spent his childhood in Greece and now lives with his family in New Jersey, received his MA degree in English from the City University of New York. He began his business career as a journalist-editor-communications specialist for various organizations—including the English section of *The National Herald*, *Metropolitan Life,* and The New York Stock Exchange. He served as the senior research editor for Fahnestock & Co. and wrote more than 100 articles for various Wall Street magazines. In 1985, he co-edited and published *A History of the Greek Orthodox Church in America.*

His literary efforts include two off-Broadway theater presentations (*Lorca* and *Three New Playwrights*) and a showcase production of the drama *SKYLLA*, centered on the lives of the Greek sponge divers of Tarpon Springs. His one-act poetic drama, *The Death of Hemingway*, was co-produced and filmed by avant-garde filmmaker Gregory Markopoulos. Christopoulos's poetry has appeared in a half dozen publications—particularly his sonnet-meditation on The Statue of Liberty. During 2001, he completed a poetic series based on his experiences during 9/11: *At the World's Tragic Center.*

MIROLOGION FROM KALAMATA

Who will care for the horse?
Who will ride him
Over the rocks and dry river bed?

Aloft on the white and black stallion,
Your massive shoulders commanded
The eye of the sky to stay open.
Your chest spoke in rhythm and
Your body absorbed the brown earth
And lifted it to the dye-blue sky . . .
When you were
Aloft on the white and black stallion.

Now those shoulders touch the earth.
Your chest is grayrock, white silence
And silent and silent and silent.
Rockwhite, silent and silent
You face the blue and the brown at once
And touch the earth with shoulders that once
Held up the blue and lifted to the sky
The outline of the brown and red earth . . .
Aloft on the white and black stallion.

Across my summer and winter
You and the Judas-star heaved forward
Like one storm-dressed cypress.
Now the tree is silent and still;
Now the great wall has fallen
And the sky and the earth have unmarried.

Who will care for the horse?
Who will ride him
Over the rocks and dry river bed?

Across my fertile spring and fall
You and the stallion galloped,
Like the storm-whipped cypress.
But the green tree is silent, silent and still:
The sky and the earth have unmarried.

And thus ... and now ... and here ...
Who will care for the neighing steed?
And who will whip back the black clouds?
Who will create the gold and the white music and ride
Bravely over the weeping rocks and the empty, dry river bed?

from *Hellenic Review*

CONSTANTINE CONTOGENIS

Constantine Contogenis's poetry collection *Ikaros* (Word Press, 2004) won a First Prize "Open Voice Poetry Award" from the Writer's Voice. He is also the co-translator of *Songs of the Kisaeng: Courtesan Poetry from the Last Korean Dynasty* (BOA Editions, 1997). He was the poet-in-residence at State University of New York, Purchase (2000-2001).

Contogenis's work has been published or is forthcoming in numerous journals such as *The Paris Review*, *Pequod*, *TriQuarterly*, *Chicago Review*, *Carquinez Poetry Review*, *Cimarron Review*, *Crazyhorse*, *Asian Pacific American Journal*, *Literary Imagination*, *Euphony*, *Lullwater Review*, *The MacGuffin*, *Western Humanities Review*, *Salamander*, *Phantasmagoria*, *Poetry East*, *New Orleans Review*, *New York Quarterly*, *Nimrod*, *Solo*, *South Carolina Review*, *Speakeasy*, *Westview*, *Whiskey Island*, *Worcester Review*, *Marlboro Review*, and *Grand Street*.

His work has also been featured by Poetry Society of America's Poetry in Motion NYC program —on the subways—and by www.versedaily.org. In a recent *Guardian* profile of Christopher Ricks, he refers to Contogenis as one of the "true poets" among contemporary writers.

Contogenis is an occasional speechwriter for the Senator Hillary Clinton campaign.

IKARIA

He remembered his body.
Thick thighs stood him shoulder-high,
fists pounded out the one shape
of his life. I asked him how
the dying was. Three fingers
pursed for the Orthodox sign
jabbed the points of garlic cloves

through white sheets of baby fat
into the leg of spring lamb
—now dressed for the flame. The room
smelled; as I kissed his forehead,
he babbled of battleships,
ocean liners, the days waiters
served water without being asked.

from *Ikaros*

THERE ARE NO PLOUGHS ON IKARIA

Since Brueghel was always right
about suffering, notice
how he gets the island wrong:
a few quick generations

split up fields to fierce gardens.
A few intolerant States
exile resisters, whom no
furrows distract from this sea.

Notice that Auden vouches
for the painting and gets it
wrong. Nothing turns away. No
man hears the cry and does not

turn. No ship sees a falling
boy and calmly does not turn.
No torturer of talent
would take work in such a place.

from *Ikaros*

THOSE MOMENTS

Let it not be those moments that matter:
last words, first sights, sickroom smells, my father
dying right. "Young doctor was angry at me,
Make up your mind, Pops, he said. *I could cut you*

a good five, ten more years. But the more you delay,
the more the knife might kill you. I wasn't sleeping right,
I told him, I'm always sleepy. *Too sleepy to decide?*
He laughed. *OK, Pops, sleep all you want.*

I liked him ... smart, funny. Asked could I pay
for his labor—*too cutting edge for Medicare.*
I have the money. Those bank CDs my family's
expecting." Am I not his family? He means

the younger ones. "I'm asking you, don't they
deserve a say? Why spend it all on a half-
chance at more life?" Dad, you fool, the hospice
brought you home, sponged you down. You're a sure thing.

Like a death, you said, leaving the sparse green island ...
your mother ... the caustic white house you're leaving
me. Those drachmas you stole from the bowl of runny
apricots to buy ice cream for friends, were dollars

your father had sent. *Blood money,* your mom said, right?
This is your father's blood. You had to be introduced
in Pittsburgh. The thick, sweet coffee settled. Then you
sprayed towers white ... served tables ... sent money home.

I tried believing you—They'd never let me write;
poems would make me too soft to fight them—
tried failing. You once heard a poem you liked,
a Communist rally, an Ikarian girl in white read:

Flowers swayed, children played—What was it?
"—the workers paid." Yes. "I thought I'd know him
but my cousins showed me. I kissed his black mustache tips.
He asked how my mother was, and I couldn't say."

Let this not be the deadline. "Did they print your book
to bring me?" No. "Well, now you'll have to live
for your daughter. That's what's left for you.
You brought her to me, that first time. Her big eyes

smiling at me. I didn't think—but the feeling was
there. Looking back at her, her hazel eyes . . . it was being
young, it was falling in love." Dad, all that time
working, saving. Now you can bring it home.

IKAROS

Before he hit, another
breathing creature timed its leap
to kiss him hard, break his skin,
teeth, nose, but blasted its own breath

to his brain, waking a taste
of salt, the knowledge of
entering the sea as he did
and last thoughts of dolphin.

Before falling, unable
to read clouds, he baited air
with feathers and sweat, was caught
by a thermal: across his

shoulders an octopus of air
sucked at the hairs of his arms,
until islands receded,
and he knew he was of age.

Before losing sight of his
father, he had stopped looking,
having no more amazement
for making, for how the man

with wings continued to shape
the air, as he let it prove
what slant of extended wings
soared, dived, and kept him in air.

Before escape, he was shamed
by flapping his arms like a
bird, by the pains, the muscles
growing inside chest and neck,

by his father's practiced change
of direction between glides,
making separate things part of
himself, himself part of things.

Before the wings were ready,
Daedalos taught him to make
glues from boiled hooves, test them
with honeycombs, and give names

to the ones stone seals could mark
but wheels could not pull apart.
With a tanning knife, he cut
the signets out of the wax.

Before their imprisonment,
he watched as his father made
oak platforms, bronze hinges, and
Egyptian ropes cease to be

metal, wood, fiber. When he
tried to catch the changes in-
to catapult or light spear,
he became too slow or quick.

Before sanctioned entry to
his father's workshop, he sought
sad girls to question, sick men
to watch die. He introduced

himself to weeping women,
was aroused to ask the names
of their loved dead. Excited,
their answers to him were signs.

Before there was a workbench,
he kept eyes to the wind until
he blinked or cried. He built walls
with holes facing the strongest

winds, wedged thin crystals, and looked
into the heart of the lung,
back at the eye, heard last breaths,
saw nothing there to be seen.

Before his father told him
the idea of windows, he
loved both sides of walls, locusts
leaving carapaces, ewes

licking newborns free of last
membranes, fish breaching the first
time, eggshells pushed in on wet
feathers, the dead in his life.

from *Ikaros*

GEORGE ECONOMOU

George Economou is the author of nine books of poetry, the latest of which are *Acts of Love, Ancient Greek Poetry from Aphrodite's Garden* (Random House, 2006), *I've Gazed So Much,* translations of Cavafy (Stop Press of London, 2003), and *Century Dead Center* (Left Hand Books, 1997). He has published many translations from ancient and Modern Greek and medieval European languages, including William Langland's *Piers Plowman* (University of Pennsylvania Press, 1996). A critic and scholar of medieval literature, he is the author of *The Goddess Natura in Medieval Literature* (Harvard University Press, 1972; reprint, University of Notre Dame Press, 2002) and numerous other books, including an edition of the late Paul Blackburn's troubadour translations, *Proensa* (University of California Press, 1978). A founding editor of *The Chelsea Review* and co-founder of *Trobar* and Trobar Books, he has published many critical reviews and essays. A Rockefeller Fellow at Bellagio, he has been named twice as an NEA Fellow in Poetry. In 2000, he retired after 41 years of teaching at the University of Oklahoma, Long Island University, and Columbia. George Economou has given readings and lectures throughout the United and States and in numerous countries abroad, such as Harvard, Princeton, Penn, Michigan, Colgate, Texas A & M, Columbia, Stanford, California, the American College of Paris, King's College of London, Oxford, and Athens, among others.

KASSANDRA'S STORY

Kassandra's story
begins where it ends,
with the gray blade
of bronze against
her throat.

[once]

The temple serpents
crept to her sleeping,
flicked their gift
upon her lips, tipping
her tongue.

[or later]

The temple's god
massaged her tongue
with his own,
then spit, when crossed,
into her mouth.

[one day]

Men would see
she was made like
the golden one,
and her forethought failed
in their ears.

[then]

Her cunt became
the prize of victors,
victims to be
of the horrors loosed
from her lips.

The blade took hold,
her life sped to the shore
of white margins,
where the glossator's wrist hangs
in the air.

from *Sulfur*

THE AMOROUS DRIFT OF THE FIRST HOPLITE ON THE RIGHT WING

The Battle of Mantinea, 348 B.C.
All armies are alike in this: on going into action they get forced out rather on their right wing, and one and the other overlap with this their adversary's left; because fear makes each man do his best to shelter his unarmed side with the shield of the man next him on the right, thinking that the closer the shields are locked together the better will he be protected. The man primarily responsible for this is the first upon the right wing, who is always striving to withdraw from the enemy his unarmed side; and the same apprehension makes the rest follow him. —Thucydides, *The Peloponnesian War*, V. 71

The amorous drift of the first hoplite on the right
wing to protect his unshielded side from the enemy
was solicitous of his survival and contagious to the
hoplite to his left whose amorous edging behind his
neighbor's shield for the sake of his survival and to
the hoplite to his left and to his left was considered
dangerous by the generals at Mantinea where both
armies having caught it moved in circuitous front lines
the Athenian phalanx the more impetuous the Spartan
though anxious to hold synchrony with the battle flutists'
pace yielding at last to the devious swerve for survival
that would be perilous if not calamitous to the generals'
plans had they not provided multifarious maneuvers
analogous to the anomalous overlapping of their left
flanks to ensure they would in the end be victorious
despite the amorous drift begun by the first hoplite on
the right wing just before the ferocious sweep into chaos.

from *American Poetry Review*

DAY OF DISEMBARKATION

It would be odd to call them Odysseys,
being outward, not homeward, bound,

lives made over by landfalls in strange cities
in spaces of magnitudes beyond magna.

Submission to a cyclopean physician
on an island more foreign than Phaeacia,

though penultimate stop of the passage,
certified the transference of homeland

and relegated Peloponnesos or Crete
to a recessive future in memory's eye,

despite a parenthetical return to bring
a woman away, not come back to her.

The couple married America and planted
a tree that would branch and burgeon into

complexions and tongues not seen or heard before
that momentous day of disembarkation.

from *The Charioteer*

AN EVENING IN KINGFISHER

"ENTERING KINGFISHER, OKLAHOMA"
the road sign reads
"THE BUCKLE ON THE WHEAT BELT."
We drive to the Elks Club
where we join three hundred men
with big buckles on their belts
to boost the Sooners & our university
in what is traditionally OSU Aggie territory
drinking & mixing with them, eating "fries"
also known as prairie or mountain oysters
scooped up barehanded
as you hold your beer or bourbon in the other
followed by steaks, ranch style baked beans
homemade cracked wheat bread & more beer
salad fixings with no dressing whatever
strong coffee & no fooling around with dessert.
After the obligatory welcome speeches
the winningest active coach in college football
runs the play he will call this spring
a hundred times throughout the state
and then fields questions:
—"Barry (pronounced Berra), how's the Texas
   game gone turn out this year?"
—"One thing I kin tell you 'bout the Texas
   game fer sure—it's gone be one tough sumabitch!"
—"Barry, could yuh use a sixty-six year old guard?"
—"Give that man another drink."
Somebody does as coach Switzer
closes this appearance with a herpes joke
and a hopeful, if not overconfident
prediction about the coming season.
The macho party & male ritual complete
(except for those with expectations
based on their consumption of fries)

we move for the doors or bartenders
and I am almost out into the night air
when the sixty-six-year-old guard pulls
out of the line at the bar & squints
at my crimson-bordered OU name tag
offering his hand to mine which he begins to squeeze
and asks me where I'm from.
—"The university."
—"Well, I kin see that. I mean with a name
   like that where are yuh *from*?"
Looking back at his tag
which reads " 'Huck' Rice"
and understanding what he's getting at,
—"Just moved here from New York,
   but I was born in Montana."
He squeezes harder,
—"But that's not an American name."
—"Sure it is, from Greece. (And making a good guess)
   When did your people come over here from
Germany, Huck?"
Easing up on the squeeze,
—"Oh hell, we bin here forever."
—"You mean you're Native American?"
—"No, no Indian. What d'yuh do at OU?"
—"I teach English."
—With a name like that, yuh teach English?"
—"I run the whole show in English, Huck.
   I'm chairman of the department, brought in
   from New York."
The handshake ends in a tie
and I am grateful for the summers
spent opening oysters in Wellfleet.
—"Well, George, how d'yuh like workin'
   here among all these Americans?"
—"I told you, Huck, I was *born* here."
—"I like yuh, George, I'd like to talk

>   to yuh 'bout your beliefs."
>
> Remembering Roy Rogers' characterization
> of Reagan when he was nominated in 1980,
> —"Why, I'm 'a fine Christian gentleman,'
>   just like you. Only my kind is the oldest,
>   Huck. Greek, you know, right back to the
>   language of the New Testament (making another
>   good guess) while you Lutherans are pretty recent."
> Shaking his head,
> —"Greek, and yuh teach English
>   and don't even have an accent."
> —"No, no accent, Huck, perfect English.
>   You've got the accent. But give me a
>   chance and I'll be back here next year
>   sounding just like you."
> —"I'd like that, I like yuh, George."
> —"So long, Huck, see you next year."
> Leaving Kingfisher, I try not to hear
> the obvious literary echoes
> and focus rather on the odd sincerity
> of my dialogue with Huck,
> and definitely name him
> to my first team offensive line.

from *Grand Street; harmonies & fits; Century Dead Center*

ELENI FOURTOUNI

Eleni Fourtouni was born in 1933, in Vassara, Laconia. She came to the US in 1952 as an exchange student. She has a BA in Social Studies and an MA in Criminology. She lives half of her life in New Haven, Connecticut, with her children, Russ and Rachel, and her grandson Kosta. The other half, she lives between her village and Aegina with her olive trees.

Her published work includes: *Greek Women Poets*, translations; *4 Greek Women*, translations; *Greek Women in Resistance: History/Journals; Watch the Flame*, original poems; *Monovassia*, original poems; and *The Return*, original poems.

Her unpublished work includes: *Chronicle of a Visit*, a novel and a work in progress; *A Trial in Athens: She Made Me Do It*, a play; *Elegy for a Lemon Tree*, a novel; and *Medea Speaks*, a dramatic monologue.

KILLING TIME

1
June
the month of the gadfly.
One two three . . . dozens of bodies.
Hundreds.
In a good day, thousands.
Who counts?
Swarms dot the windowpane.
The swatter swoops down—
once, twice, thrice,
a sharp staccato sound
like muffled gunshots
reminders of other times
when the window shutters of this house
were sawed in half and machine guns,
propped against them, disgorged fire
into the flowering fields.

After the war my mother nailed the shutters together with strips of wood,
but the crescent dents from the hot steel muzzle are still visible.

One two three . . .
Dozens alight on my legs
My arms
The corneas of my eyes—
If I let them.
Fragile.
Green-eyed.
Lidless.

A flick of the wrist is all it takes.
Dozens of bodies.
Hundreds.
Who counts?

2
Argyro said she counted twelve
twelve bodies left in the ravine—
traitors, every one of them,
hired to kill—
part of their faces missing,
the lips crab-gnawed,
flies copulating in their eyes.

They dug the graves in the field.
Argyro and four other women,
Between the plum and walnut trees,
Where now sun-bleached sheets billow over stalks of anise and balsam.

The women drove their pick axes into the earth,
They too driven,
Impaled by the indifferent sun,
Brutal as their captors.
They wrapped the rotting bodies
In lengths of linen
Meant for lace-edged bridal sheets,
Laid them in shallow graves,
Heaped over them handfuls of earth.

—*I should not be telling you, you live in this place alone.*

But she finished her story.
She knew I *had* to know
What the earth knows,
What the earth has suffered.

They butchered the herds. They sent us,
and everyone they found, to the camps.
The dogs stayed.
They got fat and lazy that June.

I should not be telling you this . . .

3
It is again June.
Balsam flowers in the meadows,
my house is whitewashed with lime,
smoked with sulfur.
A poster of a partisan
on the door she tried to storm
fifty Junes ago.
On the walls
pictures of my mother, her mother,
and her mother's mother.
Snapshots of my children crown the hearth.
My son's eyes,
the color of retsina wine,
my daughter,
like the proud-bodied woman
on a ship's prow.

They keep guard over me.

On the burial ground
I have planted a garden.
The earth has healed.

The twelve must rest in peace.

And I must intercede.
Plead for them.

4
I performed the libation at sunset:
milk and honey, wine and olive oil,
enough for a hundred traitors.
For they were children once.
Once they played tag
with those they were hired to kill,
quarreled over games of marbles with them.
Once.
Before the pestilence.

That night
the dogs returned—
Vlaha and Elli, fierce herding hounds,
descendants of a long line of bitches
born and bred
among these mountains of Lacedeamon.
Like the rest of us.

5
Traitors will have no burial.
No libation.
No forgiveness.
No peace.
—Lycourgos of Lacedeamon.

This poem refers to the civil war that erupted in Greece immediately after the country was liberated from German occupation.

THAT WOMAN SAID NO

after the "Women of Souli," by Mirtiotissa

1
I saw them
fling the children first,
like useless baggage from a sinking ship—
offerings to appease the waiting pit,
eager to commence their maniacal dance.

I saw the circle undulate,
swirl, diminish,
as one by one they unclasped hands.
And vanished.

Everyone
but you—
the very last,
standing alone,
dauntless. Mute.

Tell me,
when the song was no more,
the children's cries buried in the ravine,
when thistles and stones closed in on you—
didn't you falter then?
Wasn't death
a foe harsher than the Turk?

The others
leapt drunk with song.
You had only silence
when you faced the abyss.

Didn't terror slip into your blood then?
And when you stood at the brink,
taking the measure of the gorge,
didn't your body scream—NO!

2
When the children were gone,
and that wasn't easy—
we had to drag the older ones,
slap them—
we drew lots.

All of us wanted to be last.

No.
It was no song.
No dance.

None of us dared break out.
Our death had been decreed.

Glory . . . Freedom or Death . . .

3
No.
It was no terror.

Life wriggled out of the carnage—
a tiny silver snake
like a stream of mercury
looking for shelter.

It slipped into my blood
and I thought to linger for a while.
My eyes strayed beyond the abyss.
The moon was waning;

it would turn in a day or two,
the Pleiades hung low,
the guns were silent.
I was alone with the gorge
and the souring smell of flesh.

My death decreed.

There would be time enough for it.
I thought I'd wait for the morning star,
and for the amber mist of dawn.
Perhaps stay on,
see if the new moon would promise rain.

The women of Souli: famous for their "moment of glory," dancing to their death rather than being captured by the Turks.

UNTITLED

Now that my territory is my own
I sail alone in my bays
moor at my harbors
linger at crevices
among coral reefs that throb
at my touch—

Amber magenta garnet—
anemones of my own flesh.

Now that I have come into my own
the Earth provides—
meadows-full.
I could say I grow them myself
like the sea
with her legions
of dark phalluses
waiting in primal sludge—

Inert.

Mine
flower for my own pleasure.
the buds unfold
one after another
and the brave stem gleams—
harvest-ready.

I graze the tremulous tip—
acrid-sweet
like the loins of my last lover.
my breath
penetrates the fragile calyx—

once twice thrice …
countless entries.

No rubber dildos they,
no Priapic replicas for the amusement
of the uninitiated.

My flowering phalluses—
accessories of the imagination—
are offerings to the celibate,
to the dauntless.
To the uncompromising.

EMILY FRAGOS

Emily Fragos is the author of a book of poetry, *Little Savage*, published by Grove/Atlantic Press. Her work has appeared in *Best American Poetry*, *The New Yorker*, *American Poetry Review*, *Threepenny Review*, *Parnassus*, *Paris Review*, *Yale Review*, *Boston Review*, *et. al*. She is the editor of two anthologies of poetry from Everyman's Pocket Library: *The Great Cat* and *The Dance*. She has also written about Balanchine ballets for *Pointe* and *Bomb* magazines and wrote the libretto for Balanchine's ballet of *Don Quixote*, staged by Suzanne Farrell at The Kennedy Center, Washington, D.C., in 2005. She lives in New York City and teaches poetry at Columbia University and New York University.

SPINDLERS

Turn, she hums, and her silver pail fills with fish of snipped cloth.

Filament goes in and out of the primitive eye, is cut

By Atropos' blades. Vestments must be stitched to fit,

Cinched at the thickening waist, bodice, hips. Clotho's

Hands quiver at the choosing; Lachesis burns like ice.

One good lengthening pull and the sour body reforms

To limp, bulge, curve, hole. Spinning by dark, they

Ruin their eyes. The sisters have no use for words.

from *Barrow Street*

TO BALANCHINE

The seraphim spot you, arms splayed, eyes swollen shut,

And send the white-robed ship to find you, the walls of wave,

By its approach, nearly drowning you—sad irony for having survived

So long a frightening distance from land. Now join your suffering

To ours, chime the delirious muses, and make for us the great dance.

Mixed beings of air, earth and water with voices like laughter,

Whose faces you will never see, so covered are they by wings.

from *Barrow Street*

DAN GEORGAKAS

Dan Georgakas is a long time editor of *Cineaste* film quarterly and has guest-edited a number of special issues of the *Journal of the Hellenic Diaspora* and the *Journal of Modern Hellenism*. He is currently Director of the Greek American Studies Project of Queens College. His poetry has been anthologized in a number of collections, including *31 New American Poets, Advance Taken to Boardwalk, Abandon Automobile, A Fine Frenzy,* and *The Now Voices*. He has published *And All Living Things Their Children*, a collection of poems based on the themes and format of traditional Native American poetry and chants. Poems and fiction with explicit political themes appeared in *Three Red Stars*. He has edited three collections of poetry, translated the Greek poets Yannis Ritsos and Nikos Gatsos, and has had some of his own poems translated into German and Italian. His *My Detroit: Growing Up Greek and American in Motor City* was published in the fall of 2006.

GREEK WIDOWS OF AMERICA

Consider these Greek widows of America
completing blackclad lives
in the rented rooms of the old neighborhood
or dreaming alone in their aging homes
now that children sleep in the wedlock
so eagerly sought for them,
but which strangely had no place
for those rough-skinned peasant girls
who once were matched to older men
and now endure November graveside days
sipping the last of the homemade wine.

THE NEW JERSEY—PENWELL

is it the last black walnut tree
defying all odds? the stand of wild strawberries?
a quartet of ducklings paddling across a pond?
the stray mink? last week's skunk?
or is it the polluted musconetcong river
stirring the broken paddles of the old mill?
junked cars amid rusted beer cans?
fireflies glowing in the strip mails
like broken neon

PINBALL PURGATORIO

        I stand taut
            by the flipper buttons
of the pinball machine
          as the metal comet
               carouses in an electronic universe.
    My ego is lured by illusions
                 of perpetual play.
          Amid the clamor
              of bells, buzzers, and lights
      hope rebounds foolishly
   from bumper guard
to bumper guard.
            Flippers hurl
        and rehurl
     that hope into what seems perpetual play,
             yet, in the end, I know
                 the glittering steel must finally elude
        the straining fingers
               of my schizoid soul.

SICILIANA OF THE BYZANTINE EYES

your marsala lips evoke our history
  your windswept taormina
    and smoldering etna
  regale neglected valleys
      where ancient tongues still thrive.

your necklace of grecian temples
whispers of the golden triangle
  where europe kisses asia.

for a thousand years
  like children fresh from the womb
  we worshipped beneath egglike domes
    at your mother's ikon.

then came the zealous warriors from the east
  defiling her with their swirling calligraphy
and rigid minarets.

    it mattered not:

she passed their barriers as guilessly
  as spring eludes winter,
and on a thousand fading walls
  from my smryna to your trapani
was left the deathless legend
  of her Byzantine eyes.

FAYE GEORGE

Faye George's published collections include *Back Roads* (Rock Village Publishing, 2003), *A Wound on Stone* (Perugia Press competition winner, 2001), chapbooks *Naming the Place: The Weymouth Poems* (1996), and *Only the Words* (1995). Her poems have appeared in *The Paris Review*, *Poetry*, and numerous literary and university press periodicals and anthologies, such as *Poetry* magazine's landmark collection, *The Poetry Anthology, 1912-2002*; *Orpheus and Company: Contemporary Poems on Greek Mythology* (University Press of New England, 1999); *Poetry to Make You Smile* (MQ Publications, United Kingdom, 2005); *The Anthology of Magazine Verse and Yearbook of American Poetry*, 1980. Online appearances include: *The Endicott Journal of Mythic Arts*, *The Cultural Society*, and *Poetry Daily* (including their print anthology, *Poetry Daily*, 2003). She received the Arizona Poetry Society's Memorial Award for "Fotini" in 1986, and The New England Poetry Club's Erika Mumford Award for "The Call" in 1994. She also received the NEPC Gretchen Warren Award in 1997.

Faye George has worked as a radio copywriter, public relations representative in human services and municipal government, academic secretary, and at a variety of other jobs. She has a son, a daughter, and granddaughters, in Virginia and Connecticut. She lives in Bridgewater, Massachusetts.

KORE

Flowers drew me forth
that time when I went out
and the ground beneath my feet
fell away.

I held on to the stems
as the dark pulled me in.
Held on as if I clutched
the light of the world in my hand,
not the torn throats
of narcissus blooms.

Through the long night
in the iron earth
I clung to the fickleness
of beauty, the only candle
for the tomb.

From *Poetry*, copyright © 1991 by Modern Poetry Association; reprinted from *A Wound on Stone* (Perugia Press, 2001), copyright © 2001 by Faye George. Reprinted here by permission of the author.

THE CALL

That shop in Heraklion that sold only knives
cuts toward some association
the mind has covered with common growth.

And Pan, the goat god, leering, whittles
cross-legged, waiting for me to get the point.
I taste the spittle spuming from his pipes,

feel the coarse, curled fur of his thighs;
the sweat of his muscled chest laves me.
What does that country want?

What does it want of me, so far from the groves?
And yet so close, so close to the hot stream.

from *The Paris Review* (Winter 2000/2001)

FOTINI

I see her coming from the fields
in her widow's clothes,
the crone with her poised burden,
a shadow, a shade, a zone of mourning:
a thrum on the loom.
She is the Nana none of us knows,
the grandmother we never saw,
dead of the war, the winter hunger.

Dead of the planting and reaping;
dead of prayers and icons
and the Byzantine patience of Greek women;
dead of the sound of her own voice
against the mountain, listening for the son
who left the sheep and the goats of Olympus
for the myth of America.

I see her black kerchief folded
into the orbs of my children's eyes.
I create her face from theirs, sculpt it
like a legend out of the mountain.
It is not the face of a goddess,
it is the face of a woman, worn and spare,
the body locked in stone, chaste as tradition,
sold to a husband.

We are alone.
The almonds are in bloom.

From *The Sandcutters*, copyright © 1986 by The Arizona Poetry Society; reprinted from *A Wound on Stone* (Perugia Press, 2001), copyright © 2001 by Faye George. Reprinted here by permission of the author.

ARIS GEORGIADIS

Aris Georgiadis works as an editor for a business trade publication. His poems in this anthology are his first published works. He has a BA from New York University in journalism and is working toward an MA in clinical exercise science. When he was 10, he was convinced that he was a descendant of Alexander the Great. On more than one occasion, he curses the Fates, usually after midnight, so as not to forget his Greek ancestry. His parents were born in Greece, in the region of Macedonia—his father from Kastoria and mother from Kozani. He lives in New York.

SUMMERTIME

Dear Heart: I saw her, and my breath suddenly stilled like barbed wire.
Lithe as a fence post in the sun, her biceps tattooed with barbed wire.

Go easy, dear Heart. You beat ballistic, I'm peripatetic.
I retrace my steps on a trail of unspooled barbed wire.

Heart, I've shut the windows to the warm night, looking to cool
My wanderlust, but you smooth my cool sheets over a bale of barbed wire.

Can't you play with Memory once in awhile? She's at her loom every night,
Her tapestry vast, oppressive, open country crisscrossed with barbed wire.

I'm drunk again, Heart, enjoy this drink with me! Forget these dive
Bar maenads, meaner than rottweilers wrapped in barbed wire.

We've been in agreement before, when I sit on the bus one stop
Longer, not wanting to forget a face, my mind's eye lashed with barbed wire.

I felt you heave when we heard about Kate Hepburn. She knew
Her heart, knew of love, incorrigible, flagellated with barbed wire.

Dear Heart, I know your longing, even when wind languidly wipes
Sweat off bare skin, and the sun sits on our heads like a crown of barbed wire.

I ignore my *Lunch Poems*, Heart, for the painted gypsy in the white tank
Top and long denim skirt slit up the back, the ends frayed like barbed wire.

It's all I can do to stay as sane as a lighted window . . . I have to ignore
You, stay unpenned of your impulsiveness. My love is a starved fire,

Quit fanning the flames, Heart of mine, it's hot enough as is.
Like Aristides the Just, it's my exile to bear, across this sea of barbed wire.

ASTORIA: SESTINA

He saw his first pinup while hiding under his lean-to:
a pink, blonde and blue Miss May, an American icon
behind tomato plants in his parents' backyard in Astoria—
the grumble of the El even sounded Greek.
His blanched little city stapled in place by bridges.
Aging Delphic priestesses now wore only black to the church

underfoot the track's traverse, his relic'd church,
where he melted under altarboy robes, nowhere to lean to
keep from fainting. Now and then the subway sounded across the bridge,
oil-filled candelabras swayed over the icons
of saints, their imperturbable gazes fixed on Greek
widows who can't remember why they'll die in Astoria.

He searched for someone, anyone new to tell him a story,
but summer starched the streets silent as a church
sacristy. The nights were no relief, voices raised Greek
grieved and growled, the reek of anger leaning toward
him from behind closed doors. The moon ironed
flat against the low sky like a pinup, bridging

his mourning till morning. He trailed the dung under the bridge,
its shadow like bunting over the rattled rooftops of Astoria.
Streets and avenues teemed with faceless headstones; its idioms
rendered him mute. The oracle and the church
were of a piece, held out promises Miss May couldn't keep. Leaning to
widen his stride, his gait was as exaggerated as the Greek

alphabet. This was America, but the smells were Greek
and he followed the souvlaki stands to the Triboro Bridge.
He watched cars catch the crest of its cables leaning into
the horizon. Would the seagulls squawk the way away from Astoria's
idolaters, their directions becoming his crutch
inscribed with the rubric of iconoclasts

who spoke in tongues, whose veins blued with the ichor
of doubt and desire? No longer would the sound of Greek
make him tremble, no longer would he seek asylum in churches
made of wax and rosewater. He would bridge
his moated history and keep his feet dry of tears after leaving Astoria,
never to count the weeks by liturgy and Lent.

He knelt in prayer, leaning to leave a votive on the icon
in the shape of his voice. Leaving Astoria, the writing on the wall was
    still Greek,
and all the time he'd bridge still wouldn't outlast the Church.

VERONICA GOLOS

Veronica Golos is the author of *A Bell Buried Deep*, co-winner of the Nicholas Roerich Poetry Prize (Story Line Press), whose poems were nominated by Edward Hirsch for a 2004 Pushcart Prize. She was a finalist for the Ann Stanford Prize and for the Tupelo Press Prize. In both 2003 and 2005, she was the recipient of a three-month long artist's residency at the Wurlitzer Foundation of Taos, New Mexico. She is also the author of the chapbook, *No Ordinary Women*. Presently, she is working on a new book of poems inspired by the Southwest, *Intimate Red*.

Golos teaches poetry and multi-genre writing for *Poets & Writers*, Poets House, and 92nd St Y/Makor. Along with writer Connie Josephs, she is writing, *The Use of Years: Writing Your Life*, a guidebook for writing memoirs.

Her poems have appeared in *Rattapallax, Writers Voice, Long Shot, Natural Bridges, Callaloo, Drunken Boat, BigCityLit, Bridges—a Jewish Feminist Journal, Poets Corner, Long Island Review, Poetry London, Orion, Chokecherries, Gathering of the Tribes*, and *Zeek* among others. Her work also appears in *Southern California Anthology, Ophelia's Mom, A Time of Trial: Beyond the Terror of 911*, and *3poets4peace*, the poems of which have been translated into French for the journal *Liquor44*.

A BELL BURIED DEEP

Feasting on the aftertaste,
I weaken first,
rise, stand at the window—
my pale skin flushed in the North Carolina light.
The old wood planks moan,
the white bedspread ripples like new snow,
our white sheets are the color of white beneath white—
and you, your brown skin against the sheet,
our marriage the color of syrup.

I lift my eyes and am chastened
by the angry heartbreak this world can bring.
The treetops are tender green—
and what is the color green but everything washed clean,
even the tiny, blue stone cemetery
where my son remains . . .
does not rise, even after this, his eleventh year.
He is blue in the ground, his light-blue bones,
the midnight cap of his hair, his infant smell—
a bell buried deep, where he was in me,
ringing, ringing.

My god,
love making
can redeem
but does not release
pain! I do not forget
my periwinkle boy, my blue berry, my demon—
all his names in a world pulsing with names,
wild christenings in the air—
as the blue-green vein of my wrist beats,
the memory of him, our pale-boned boy,

drives me back to our bed
to touch you, his dark father,
with my grief full of tongues,
full with his name.

from *Rattapallax* and the collection of the same name

RE-TURN
after Matt Pasca's Dead of Winter

I crouch on a throne of singular bone
picking pomegranate seeds from my teeth.

One was enough; now it doesn't matter
how many I eat—rules being what they are:

I'm bride till spring.

Above, at the place I was taken,
waits my childhood basket, stiff as a ring.

The Narcissus I tugged at
still clings, collecting its cupfuls of dew.

Down here, I speak with the most recent dead;
They age towards transparency, you see:

the hands, then the head, a final stare—
till I'm talking to air.

Even so, I repeat
the classic story, my capture, my screams,
reread from the reams of my mother's

appeals. Then, the temperature rises;
I claw through the floor, pry open the door

straight into the frosted ground;
I come out by going around and

backward: body into intention; desire
into the dash of quick green grass.

HOLLYHOCK LOVE SONG

Their white pink red mouths
stretch to the sun.
They nod and lean like graceful dancers,
stems longer than a woman's arm
reaching for her partner's hand.

One thick thumb of a bee
rubs itself into the apron
of a flower; its whole yellow self
shakes and trembles as it dives
 into the wild latitude of pollen.

The sunlight is so clear.

Each morning I wake to you,
heart of fire, crossroads, quiet
burning timber of soul.
Your words are sparks of campfire
sent to loosen the tight knit stars.

How long I have loved you.
You are the air between my fingers.

You walk in my river,
wade deep, never leave. Your legs
are the gallon legs of horses, your
arched back the gold earth of the Plains.

Right outside our door,
the Hollyhocks aim their faces heavenward;
a bit of flame, caught, inside their core.

PERSEPHONE OF DEMETER

Her hair had withered on its stalk.
Her words were nothing but salt.
What could I know of grief?

I took the eye-shaped seed
placed it in my mouth—
the world I knew folded
over my head;
I descended into the dream
of this desert place
where the stones open their cuts
and show their blood-tinged skin.

DEMETER TO PERSEPHONE

There was nothing I gave you did not take;
Nothing I had you did not overthrow.

Hold you now, as I never could?
In calling you, what word was it I forgot?

What does it take to stop loving the world?
Stand in the corn and see what I see:

You leaving me.

M.J. GOLIAS

M.J. Golias is originally from Massachusetts. She did her BFA at Emerson College, her MA/MAT at Rivier College, and then her MFA in poetry at the University of Memphis, where she was awarded a teaching assistantship and scholarship. She teaches English in the New York City public schools and writes poetry and creative nonfiction. Poems of hers have appeared in various literary journals. Her constant influences are Ritsos, Seferis, and the Polish poets Adam Zagajewski and Wiswala Szymborska. She lives in New York City.

THE OLIVE GROVE

points west where the sun
settles in dry land. You swim
in cerulean only on weekends.
Schools of black small fish
slide along boats' grimy

sides. Your hands are pitted
Kalamata olives—blue veins
threaded. Your hands your living
nurturing bright green *karpouzia*
round like the beginnings of a baby

growing inside its mother.
I never saw your face.
I watched your hands hold
the watermelon handing it over
to us. The air is fishnet

as we stand in the patch wanting
what isn't ours. We are impatient—
umbrella sun with watermelons.
Thirst chokes, enfolds, wrinkles
in the arid heat. I think

of you as Yorgos smashes
the *karpouzi* onto the pavement
after your back is turned. We feast
with hands, digging with fingers,
even eating seeds.

GHAZAL

Who will account for those not freed because of the diaspora?
Return the labor of their need because of the diaspora?

The children of the children forget history, aged and empty coffins.
Families fled with throats that couldn't breathe because of the diaspora.

Air hangs like a newly butchered lamb in a restaurant.
How soon after did men and women take heed because of the diaspora?

Listen: dissolve not in salt, walk out sunned. Assimilation is exile.
Tell me the names that took the lead because of the diaspora.

Tell me names, whisper to Maria—because of the diaspora
she is here. Ancestral wounds are now seeds because of the diaspora.

TRANSLUCENT HOMELANDS

He asks if I am part gypsy,
there in the face it shows.
Miles of caravans inside me

for centuries. Must answer the question
of why I can't plant roots.
No, not necessarily.

Just before the fruit and vegetable markets
I find letters inside me that never get written,
never mind sent, and always mentioned

to someone who doesn't care. I look for
granite to anchor me. I look for
signs in the few trees that line these

New York City streets—no threat
of monsoons to carry me somewhere else.
I tell him: Gypsies came from India

a thousand years ago; they found Europe
and mixed, and quite possibly in Asia Minor
with someone in my family. Now it's an insult

to accuse of such things.
Yes, I know, something in my face.
Desperation, like rumors, spreads.

Desolation hides on ocean fronts
in pretense of offering
refuge from the madness—such

bountiful breaks in the water,
in the many ships that promised
to carry me to a home.

STATHIS GOURGOURIS

Stathis Gourgouris was born in Hollywood and grew up in Athens. He has published four volumes of poetry, one in English (*Myrtle Trenches*, 1985) and three in Greek: Πτώσεις (Plethron, 1988), Αυτοχθονίες (Planodion, 1993), Εισαγωγή στη Φυσική (To Melani, 2005). He has translated into English the poetry of Yiannis Patilis and Argyris Chionis and into Greek the poetry of Carolyn Forché and Heiner Müller. His translations of his own poetry into English have appeared in *The Harvard Review, The Jacaranda Review, Compages, LA Weekly, Emergences, Modern Poetry in Translation, Mondo Greco,* and in various anthologies of Greek poetry, most recently in *A Century of Greek Poetry (1900-2000)*, edited by Peter Bien et al. (Cosmos Publishing, 2004). His work has been translated in French, Italian, Serbian, and Turkish. He is currently professor of comparative literature at UCLA. The following poems first appeared in the book *Autochthonies*.

POSEIDONIANS (*FIN DE SIÈCLE*)

I

We live in a peculiar time.
Around us gather heaps
of unknown translucent nights.
Within us flicker stories of life.
Before us, a visible black star
more black than the most red
more visible than the most deep.

(Someday, the national poets will name us
myth-divers vanquished by myth.)

There was a time we mastered
the infinitives of matter.
The substantives were lost.
Such voyages, such worlds
with mind forever flowing
not toward maps but verbs
toward the algebra of the flesh
the salt of sadness.

Captives of coincidence—
in other words:
gramophones out of control
Bedouins whose horse is the phrase of God.

II

As Greeks, we left behind
lonely and homeless columns
turning to face the sea
like still-voiced women.

To strangers we showed
what psyche means, what is infinity.
Without a compass, without purgatory
(foreign inventions)
we took to the dark seas
out of sheer fondness
for studying stars.

Eventful ruins never caught up with us,
no matter what they say, how they admonish us,
these poets of misfortune.
Such catalytic fraud was known already
to the irascible Heráclitus—
that lyric goddess of the desert
who cast a spell upon Berlin.
To her we light these fires
on Patagonian rocks,
throwing all passwords to the sea
along with the grand shadows raised
by walls collapsing.

Indians always of our own dreams.
With a window flung open in our memory
so as to call on a few trees
on a few birds
a salty breeze over the branches
leafing through wrinkled pages of time.
An earsplitting silence.

FOR KÓRINNA *(6TH C. BC)*

A woman waits at the edge of the world for her life to turn the page. She waits for the stone to gain its fly-leaf, for two whole words to fold over Time who sits upon a chasm. Her life is a poem erasing itself from inside out, slow and without trace. Her soul unwraps the amber veil of oblivion from the spindle of love. The words, in love with oblivion, gradually swallow the interstices, cough up time to the void, forget the body twice folded in a sheet of paper forging a trace on truth. Words forget bodies, become one with the paper—they oxidize it, they give it breath, they expiate it. And letter by letter, they expire. From inside out, from the center of the soul to the margins of matter. A woman at the edge of time waits. To see the history, if she can, behind the chasm. History counts time with chasms. Time counts each chasm with a poem.

THE DREAM OF PENELOPE DELTA

The book cover of my pain
a smile that bound me tightly
as one morning
a bullet struck
love's infertile breath.

You died as when I first met you.
Dressed in your linen suit
a naked country's
monarch in rags.

DIVER IN LOVE WITH OBLIVION

I throw myself
bait
to sleep.
I sink at once.
I dangle handsome
irresistible
before the eyes
of desperate
fish.

I unhook myself.

At night
I carry my dreams
in fish crates.

THEA HALO

Thea Halo's first career was as a painter. She attended The Cooper Union School of Art and Architecture and has shown her paintings in galleries and museums in New York City, Connecticut, and Canada, including both solo and group exhibitions. Her paintings are in collections in the US and abroad. Halo also attended the City University of New York and was awarded a fellowship.

Beginning in 1992, Halo worked as an announcer and producer for Public Radio. In 1996, Halo wrote her own column for a weekly newspaper in upstate New York, and beginning in 1997, she worked as a news correspondent for public radio station WBAI in New York City, gathering, writing, and reporting the five to seven minute news stories in the public radio tradition.

In 1992, Halo began to write poetry and short stories, and soon after commenced the writing of her mother's memoir, *Not Even My Name*, published in 2000 by Picador USA, an imprint of St. Martin's Press. She has won numerous awards for her poetry, and her literary and political essays.

NIGHT

Near dawn
my eyelids have still not surrendered.
Shadows on the ceiling,
cast by street lamps,
echo objects without a quiver.

I can almost hear the snowflakes
knot like lace on city streets,
and a few hushed footsteps
incise the newly tatted snow.
Then the whir of trucks
collecting the refuse of other lives.

Funny how they wait like thieves
until all are sleeping,
then rattle and clatter and rumble
loud enough to wake the innocent.

What gifts were discarded today
that once were meant to meld two hearts?

I know what I've given you.
But what have you received?

Last night a friend called.
He told me of a poet's dream;
a dream in which a sheep came.
Gracious as she was
she did not scold.
"I heard you had my lamb for dinner,"
she said. "God bless you.
How did you enjoy
the flesh of my child?"

And again I'm transported
to my mother's land.
I hear the soldier shout,
"Throw it away if it's dead,"
as her mother holds up her dead child
for the soldier to see.

And again I resurrect them,
erasing the sunken cheeks and hollow stares
that mar her family's youth and beauty.
I clothe them in their Pontic dress,
and send them to play in the fields again
among the wildflowers and cows
beneath their sentinel sky,

as my sky brightens.
The shadows on the ceiling fade.
But even when my eyelids close
my eyes maintain their vigil,
traveling many roads.

How many histories
will I carry to my grave?

"I know what I've given you ..." is from a poem by Antonio Porchia (1885-1968).
"A dream in which a sheep came ..." alludes to a poem by Hovhannes Tumanian (1869-1923).

GIFT OF THE GODS

They gave me eyes
and too many senses
Sent me on journeys
from Ithaka and back
Gave me muses
language
and time
to whittle this Sisyphean life
into art
Then they handed me the reins
tied to a stone

NICHOLAS JOHNSON

Nicholas Johnson is cofounder and Senior Poetry Editor of *Big City Lit*, the literary magazine at bigcitylit.com, and co-producer of the 2002, 2004 *Lyric Recovery Festival* at Carnegie Hall. He is a MacDowell Colony fellow, Pushcart Prize nominee, and winner of the *Lyric Recovery Festival Poetry Award 2000* at Carnegie Hall (Dana Gioia, judge). Johnson's degrees include an MFA in poetry from Brooklyn College and an ABD from the Catholic University of America. He has taught there and at the College of New Rochelle. He has appeared in *The Word Thursdays Speaking the Words Tour and Festival* in Delaware County and, for the past three summers, has co-organized a series of readings and workshops in juvenile detention facilities, at libraries, and elsewhere in rural Greene and Albany Counties. Johnson's poetry has been published in *Confrontation*, *Shenandoah*, *American Poetry Review*, *Rattapallax*, *Epoch*, *The Journal*, *The Ledge*, *Pivot*, *Poetry Wales*, *Mudfish*, *American Letters & Commentary*, the *Anthology of Magazine Verse & Yearbook of American Poetry*, and *Chance of a Ghost* anthology.

He has taught Creative Writing for many years at The Payne Whitney Clinic and The Lighthouse in New York City. His new chapbook, *Degrees of Freedom*, is now available from Bright Hill Press.

BACK HOME

Nothing much has changed. The insects
ping against the bellied screen that then
stayed open more than closed, swung
creaking and snapped back like those doors
will do that belong mostly to the poor.
Swung by children and the ones who'd rather
not porch it, yet know of the attendant charm,
rocker and swing, watching the light settle
down into another evening as the guns
of Aberdeen boom out to remind us—
this is still the 20th century. The acres
of corn look more under water every day,
and August is souring the hay with unexpected
rain. The one you'd like to talk to
is sitting with the rest and there are two
lanterns on the table and the folks sit
around hunching and sprawled in a turn
that suits them. You might have considered it
a triumph on another day to fall asleep
with your face in your plate, with all
the heat bugs whining tomorrow's weather.
About the time someone takes out their teeth
to get comfortable, the lights are going out.
Up in that damp bed, you are lying there
as if you knew there were no good reason to go back
where you came from, or to go on, and no
possibility of doing either, but still
not wanting to close your eyes, to bed down
in that perpetual-for-the-night way,
which is what you ought to be doing
if you ever want to look at the morning
like it was going to be morning, and not
the beginning of the same old day.

from *Confrontation; The Hudson Pier Poets: Ten Years by the River; Degrees of Freedom*

POINT OF HONOR

If I loved honor more, there'd be more dead people.
My father's shotgun would have been used
not just on himself or as an impressive wall ornament.
If I loved honor more, there'd be more people hurt
for stupid reasons. My wife would have been shot
in the act, her lover in the back, all
because of an exchange of bodily fluids.
Yes, she'd have come to me with her legs and knees
all bandaged up, asking for money and forgiveness—
the things I'm running out of. If I loved honor more,
I'd have done my full stint in my jet fighter,
shot anything that moved, and not felt bad about it.
I'm still not clear on all the points of honor.
I was stupid for a long time—longer than I was married,
longer than I hoisted a flag. Take a look around. Look
how many are dead. If honor had been involved,
there would have been more: Fisticuffs. Duels. Seconds.
Honor has made people happier than alcohol.
If honor were involved, there would be no World
Trade Center left at all. No business as usual. Me,
I'm sick of bodily fluids and scraping things off
after C-4's done its work. I'm sick of the air
that insults our lungs, and all that's thrown at us
on the evening news. We should know better than to
consume ourselves and moralize. Thank God for death.
The ability to put ourselves in someone else's shoes
we don't even know. The enemy is a shadowy character.
There are too many silent partners. Buddy, I know,
because I was one of them for a long time. Like most men,
I've borne my share of coffins down, but if I had to
choose, I'd rather listen to a band no one had to march to.

from *Poetry Wales; Big City Lit; Degrees of Freedom*

SMOKING VILLANELLE

You sit and smoke another cigarette.
You pray each time you feel the end is near.
How many miracles can you expect?

I miss the cross you wore around your neck.
I know sometimes you think that God can hear.
You sit and smoke another cigarette.

You've suffered from attention and neglect.
It's hard to see you, shaking, full of fear.
How many miracles can you expect.

You know the things you love, you must protect.
Take a deeper breath. Wipe away the tear.
Sit down and have another cigarette.

I know you count on things you can't forget:
The smoky rooms, the music in your ear,
how many miracles you can expect.

We're here today. Gone somewhere else the next.
The church bells always ring at noon. Ring clear.
Sit down, love. Have another cigarette.
How many miracles can you expect?

from *Rattapallax; Degrees of Freedom*

POOR COMPANY

The man at the bar asked me why
I looked depressed. My wife just died,
I told him. I don't know why
he asked. I don't know why I told him
my wife died. Maybe I was glad.
Maybe I didn't have a wife. Never, or
not anymore. Maybe I didn't tell him
my wife died. Maybe I wasn't depressed.
Maybe he was gay. Maybe I was gay.
Maybe there was no man at the bar
and I invented him for company. Maybe
I didn't like his company, so he disappeared.
Nobody has seen him since.
That was my good deed for the day.
I promise you, that man, so full of concern,
that man won't bother anyone again.

from *Rattapallax; The Second Word Thursdays Anthology; Degrees of Freedom*

GEORGE KALAMARAS

George Kalamaras is the author of six books of poetry, four of which are full-length, *Gold Carp Jack Fruit Mirrors* (The Bitter Oleander Press, forthcoming 2008), *Even the Java Sparrows Call Your Hair* (Quale Press, 2004), *Borders My Bent Toward* (Pavement Saw Press, 2003), and *The Theory and Function of Mangoes* (Four Way Books, 2000), winner of the Four Way Books Intro Series. He has also published poems in numerous journals and anthologies in the United States, Algeria, Canada, Greece, India, Japan, Mexico, Thailand, and the United Kingdom, including *The Best American Poetry 1997*, *American Letters & Commentary, The Bitter Oleander, Boulevard, Epoch, Hambone, The Iowa Review, New Letters, Sulfur, Talisman, TriQuarterly*, and others. Professor of English at Indiana University-Purdue University Fort Wayne, where he has taught since 1990, Kalamaras is the recipient of Creative Writing fellowships from the National Endowment for the Arts (1993) and the Indiana Arts Commission (2001), as well as first prize in the 1998 *Abiko Quarterly* International Poetry Prize (Japan). During 1994, he spent several months in India on an Indo-US Advanced Research Fellowship from the Fulbright Foundation and the Indo-US Subcommission on Education and Culture. Three of his four grandparents emigrated to the US from Greece in the early 1900s: George Avgerinos from the Ionian island, Zakynthos, and Pericles and Stavroula Kalamaras (Demopoulous) from Pharaklatha, Kyparissia and Solike, Messinia.

IN THE CAFÉ OF STRANGE SKIN

In the café of strange skin, some woman or other was always staring vacantly into me as if she belonged to Delvaux. I had been a curator, that lifetime, in New Delhi, just back from a book-buying expedition in Lisbon. When I opened the moon, the train platform roared as if surrounded in birds, as if I was no longer alive, bitten by bees, and returned to my sorrowful bed of straw. It was a situation unlike no other, and I did not want to repeat it, even though I craved Greek pastry, *galaktoboureko* or *halvah*. In the café of strange skin, I was under the cruel influence of coffee. I had been star-bitten, hard, and required anything remotely bitter to calm me down. Absorbed in raking gravel through the chest cavity of a crow, I was beside myself with a contact of small friends. Even the squirrel knew my name in Maharashtran meant *school of established mustaches*. I required a requiem, requisite medicines found only in the bone-worship practiced by seasoned elephants. I needed the ancestor's tired tusk passed trunk to trunk among the herd, sniffed—after a year of death and great migration—for the proper flea scent and yeast. I opened the bite bitten into me by bees, in the café of strange skin. I wondered why they bit and did not sting, why each lamp-bearing nude reclining in the almost-pleasure moan of every conceivable position belonged only to me.

from *Barrow Street*; reprinted in *Even the Java Sparrows Call Your Hair* (Quale Press, 2004)

BANARAS IS ANOTHER NAME FOR THE WORLD

A sadhu carries a lamp to the Ganges,
unwinds his long hair into the river.

The Milky Way glitters in mud, twigs,
snags of carp, and ashes of millions.

Were they content over the evening dal?
Did they like tea? How were they touched?

Banaras is another name for the world.
Ganga, for the mother of the world.

You count the goats on the steps
of the bathing ghat and consider a new profession.

Maybe the chai wallah understands
the goats better than the goatherd?

New constellations form in the pail. Sagittarius
is not a mineral deficiency detailed in stools.

Whenever opposites attract, cobblestones shift a little and
the street curves inward at an almost undetectable slope.

You wander old Muslim neighborhoods on Madanpura on your
way to Chowk, sense the love of God even in cooking meat.

See how smoke from cremation grounds speckles the river?
You want to step in but you've seen the dead cow.

You've seen the purple corpse when you took the boat.
You've seen the men urinating against the wall.

Where is the gold carp and where is your foot?
How might you bathe in the river without getting in?

from *The Bitter Oleander*, reprinted in *Vespers: Religion & Spirituality in Twenty-first Century America*

PARTHENOGENESIS

At that time we had heard of Krishna and the Gopis.
We found ourselves surrounded on all sides by green bath rugs.

Some evenings I become Athens.
I ask a shoemaker whether autumn will ever return.

Then I strictly my sleep.
You cannot locate my name, pristine, in the parthenogenetic dust.

I have kept a raincoat so long, my hamstring is tight.
Write a sonnet, but balance it as an optional cave.

Whom have I eaten when I slurp the nostalgia of snow?
There is a hexagon paw-printed in my other chest.

It is so sweet, the way Krishna loves each Gopi for whom she is not.
I find myself at night, parallel to the in-between.

from *The Bitter Oleander*

ON THE DEATH OF MILTOS SAHTOURIS

1919-2005

So now I will never meet you, Miltos Sahtouris.
So, a long time from now, July 29, 1919 will forever be inscribed backwards as my shame.

I will never arrive at your tiny Athens apartment, hat in trembling hand.
You will not open the door, squinting me my size, and tenderly hand me a fish covered in owl feathers, saying, *Surrealism freed me from many things.*

But let's say we *did* meet.
Let's say we sat smoking and that you opened a vein and out came Ethiopian coffee.

Let's say the mug held blood.
That in the grounds the poems of Andreas Embericos and Nikos Engonopoulos kept soaking like rags in kerosene.

And Miltiades—let me call you *Miltiades*, just once, reclaiming from the crows your name at birth—let's say that we went hand in hand to Hydra to piss on the grave of your great, great grandfather, giving the old war Admiral warm water for his bones.
Let's say the entire island turned out to see that in his chest he still carried a goat, that the War for Independence could never entirely be struck from this bone or that.

Like this sliver of eel fire the birth bag burst to become my brain.
Like the weight of Cavafy luring us all to some dark Alexandrine corner and trembling hand.

On my shelf, alphabetized in the manner of fire or fish, your books separate Ritsos from Seferis.
I see you as a kind uncle, keeping the boys from biting one another's wrist, instructing them on the merits of a tiny cot in a tiny Athens apartment

where one sits day after day eating tiny cookies from the little neighborhood confectionery on the corner.

It has been written that in your *Poems, 1945–1971* you cite precisely 526 colors in 234 pages, that the colors black (105), red (82), and white (56) predominate.

It has also been written—but never publicly revealed—that in my dream of meeting you, there are 453 animals silently roaming the room where we sit together and smoke, that in 1 hour, 43 minutes of my dreaming the owl appears (1 hour, 13 minutes, 53 seconds), then the donkey and rooster (16 minutes, 53 seconds and 12 minutes, 11 seconds, respectively), and finally the bearded child (a fleeting 3 seconds).

So now it is getting late, Miltos Sahtouris, and all this dreaming adds up to the truth that I can never dream, can never quite color the sky—that is—the same Chagall-horse blue.

You are dead or dying or about to crumble into your great, great grandfather's bones or about to be reborn as some poisonous butterfly from Ethiopia or Peru or Mount Athos itself, and we will never meet, my friend, and a lace-trimmed wing will part the sea-lice on my chest as I stand on the shore and sing, and a long time from now we will still never meet.

LOOKING FOR MY GRANDFATHER WITH ODYSSEAS ELYTIS

I'm walking through the narrow lanes of Athens and Elytis is at my side, his right arm looped through my left. His bald head, involved in some secret triangulated message-sending with the full moon and sunken sun. We are searching for the grandfather I grew up with, George Avgerinos, though he has been dead twenty-six years. *Not here, not here*, Elytis says, gently patting my hand, when I lean into a corner, when I crane my neck into the retsina scent of a taverna, salivate on the street near a woman in black and the open spit for a lamb, remembering my Nono, my brother Perry, and me dividing the tongue into three even parts. And though I don't believe him, I know he must be right.

Then we're in Zakynthos, the island of my grandfather's birth. "The Poet's Island" Dionysius Solomos made famous in 1822 and that now forever holds his name. Somehow we've left Athens and have crossed the Ionian. Moonlight resembles an asphalt bridge, lava floes of solidified sulfur at Minerva Terrace in Yellowstone. I look back and watch them dissolve in lapping caps and leaping hagfish. A Greek Orthodox priest emerges from a glass coffin. He has seaweed on his slippers. He wears a tiny gold cap; I sense that he is bald. He's Saint Dan, greeting us in demotic, saying something about *hair shirts* and *stones in the mouth at Mount Athos* and *retsina wind carving cliffs* and *lamb's tongue tucked safely in the chest of every newborn foal.* His censer floats through Elytis, and Elytis's cigarette suddenly catches moon-flint and lights. *Not here*, he coughs, that hearty, tuberculous cough of the many-smoked, thick clouds soaking us both, the lava floes reemerging then disappearing within the rasping strokes of the hagfish.

We thank Saint Dan, kneel and kiss his feet. I hear something about *my son* and *good boy* and *mind that tongue in your own chest now too.* Somehow both he and Elytis know my secret. That solstice night in Colorado nineteen years ago when I kissed the back cover photo of Elytis from *Maria Nephele* before writing poetry, before logging the first vowel. And then before sleep, kissing it again, slipping it beneath my pillow, holding my right index finger over the outline of his mouth as I curled into the darkness.

Drops of light, drops of light, I had silently chanted, echoing Elytis's core, into moon-folds of sleep, into the sunken yet persistent sun. And now both Saint Dan and Elytis look at me, each clasping two hands together in air as makeshift pillows and, standing, rest their heads upon them, saying in chorus, *Drops of light, Giorgos. Vowel without end, Giorgos. Tongue in the chest.*

Saint Dan returns to his coffin, caressing the hasp, seaweed stains on the stones. Elytis takes me deeper into the island to a small village, a two-room hut. My great-grandmother, Angeline, is on the floor, the midwife spreading olive oil on her crotch. Pans of boiled water. The lantern carving out notches on the wall. *Here, Odysseas?* I ask, self-conscious that I've called him by his first name. First the kiss, now nineteen years later assuming the liberty of his Christian name? He pats my hand, saying only my name in Greek, *Giorgos*. I remember the gamey taste of tongue, eating it with my grandfather, asking why it was I who got his name. My great-grandmother moans, moon-flint again catching Elytis's cigarette. Something like a lava floe stains the birthing rug. It is beautiful and terrible. My great-grandmother's face tightened as in orgasm or broken bones. I want to cry out, save her, but I have no voice. Each time I go to speak, the ash on Elytis's cigarette glows more brightly, and something in my chest elongates through waves of saliva, crushing my heart, caressing my esophagus, flaring pinkish folds against my lungs. The midwife is now a giant fish, black shawl clasping the damp. Fierce gills pumping night wind, forcing some rasp in the shape of, *Push, push!* Elytis holds my hand, measures his breath to mine. He gently undoes my trousers, the buttons of my shirt, dabs sweat from my brow, rubs olive oil on my groin, in slow circles at the sensitive tip of my penis, on my chest just above the nipples where the crushing begins. *Push, push*, he says. *Vowel without end in the chest*, he says. *Soon you will speak, Giorgos. Soon you will speak.*

from *Luna*; reprinted in *No Boundaries: Prose Poems by 24 American Poets*; reprinted in *The Drunken Boat*; reprinted in *Even the Java Sparrows Call Your Hair* (Quale Press, 2004)

NINA KARACOSTA

Nina Karacosta is from Athens, Greece. She has a BSc in Physics from the University of Patras. She then followed her passion for theater and studied drama in Webber Douglas Academy of Dramatic Arts in London. She came to New York in 1995 and continued her studies in acting, followed by performances. The last three years, after studying poetry at the Poetry Project, she discovered her poetry within the perplexing English language. She's always trying to make peace between her first influences of the immense worlds of Cavafy and Seferis, the French surrealists, and her current exposition and fascination with experimental and performance poetry.

DREAM

Inside the dark lights light dark
theater space
quietude

on the left my friend X
a wavering in our walk
a tower   a moon   a nostalgia.

He says:
there—on the rolling black of a stage
a gather of   fools
will eat up the air with peculiar words
powdered eyelids
gestures and mimics.

My uncle Toulis stands in front of me
his mouth surprised
"Yes you were here last year uncle weren't you?"

Eyes on my tiger step, step turn arrival
in the first raw
where I create exile.

I fall hopeless in the exodus where
a woman messenger
orders me to follow her
inside a microscope.
See: my mom's new farmhouse
see: the kitchen's delirious yellow floor

why would she shape a color like that?
see: there are no pictures of me.

Elsewhere, in the garden: bees.

NOSTOS

Photographer paints the stone
Plunge
Time is for the time it was.

my face   a kid
        wet stamp   map   train in the countryside
  sleep   the eyes of hawk
his face   glasses   well-shined shoes
        his watch   waistcoat   dividers
  mechanical pencil
my face   an afternoon
        boldness
his face   the empire
        decompressed spiral
my face   the silent dancing of stone   the tremble of wind
his face   *all my remaining life* he said

behind my face the cunning of small gods
behind his face 1922   and the sea East where he comes from
                                                  Black Sea
                  they haven't kept his home   they
  haven't kept his home

Smoke, black soup, teeth
prayer notes
intense prayer notes next to bicycle music.

SOLITAIRE

I open up and sustain any pain.
One milligram, a kilo, a tone, an ounce. Any
pain, any drug brought to me now will be tasted irredeemably.
I will shout all the names of insects –
I will say: *grasshopper, beetle, maybud, ant, butterfly, caterpillar*
    mosquito, cricket, firefly, gnat, moth, spider, daddy longlegs.
I will then wet a biscuit and place it next to
yellow cheese. I don't eat but I observe. I
am ready. The days run one next to the other.
Fall arrives. The cat walks around the yard. She's
ready. There are postcards on my wall that chit-chat
endlessly. Their blue-green water in the night
becomes purple. The water is ready. Even if
I'm not dead, old parts of me are dead
and I miss them terribly. My tears are silver.
My tears cut a ditch across the train rails.
I can't travel. I'm mysteriously lost in
a world of misconceptions. I add
numbers day and night in a logarithmic paper.
I smoke fat green puffy cigarettes and
I exhale little vowels in the air. I sleep
and sleep and sleep until my eyes are
muggy. I dream of escape. Day and night
I draw maps and color them. I am not
me because if I were I would know what
I'm not. All this adds up to nothing. To suspend.

PENELOPE KARAGEORGE

A prize-winning poet, Penelope Karageorge's work has appeared in numerous journals ranging from *Literal Latte* to *A Room of Her Own* and *Mondo Greco*, as well as anthologies including *The Literature of Work* (University of Phoenix Press) and *Proposing on the Brooklyn Bridge* (Grayson Books). Her first poetry collection, *Red Lipstick and the Wine-Dark Sea*, was published by Pella. She is the author of a crime novel, *Murder at Tomorrow* (Walker Publishing), and *Stolen Moments* (Pinnacle Books), a satirical romance and roman à clef set in the magazine world, published in England as *Winners*, and in Germany as *New York*. She has made short films and written feature length screenplays, including *Drinking the Sun*, set on the Greek island of Lemnos. A die-hard New Yorker, she is equally in love with Lemnos and frequently visits the stone house there that she inherited from her grandmother, Sevaste. Born in Newburgh, New York, she is a graduate of Simmons College, Boston, Massachusetts, and earned an MA from the City University of New York. A freelance journalist whose work has appeared in publications including *Cosmopolitan*, she contributes frequently to *Odyssey* magazine. She began her career as a *Newsweek* reporter interviewing luminaries including Jane Fonda, Cary Grant, Bette Davis, and Frank Sinatra, and was publicity director of *People* magazine.

AVENUE "B" REMBETIKO

In the East Village restaurant with the jazz
clarinetist blowing people in from the street,
I talked with Dean about the LSD trip, how the
ocean exploded in light, and a warm paper plate
burned my hand, and my face turned crone-haggard.

Hardship traveled from Greece with
them. Tragic eyes set them apart,
guests in this Lana-Turnered landscape
of America. But I, fed on Rice Krispies and
speaking no other tongue than English, was
anointed to go forth smiling, although
my first loves were foreign and solemn,
ancient black-dressed ladies with paper
sacks who dug in dirt for dandelion
greens, and taught me to sop up
olive oil from a plate rimmed with bluebirds.

Young? I did not know the art. How hard
I practiced being young, finding role models
in films and *Photoplay*. Liz showed me how
to pose, chin tilted up, Debby to dance,
and *Seventeen* the secrets of teen-think
and talk, what to tell "Dear Diary," instant
teenager in bobby sox and Revlon Love That Red.

Years later, on LSD, my face alarmed a fellow
tripper who saw me transmogrify. The mask
slipped and the truth burst through,
like patched clothes popping from
a cardboard suitcase tied with string.

EXILE

When I return to my Greek house in the village
        of Lichna, the stones await me.
I swallow them with salt and greens and weep.
        Yiayia, I live in your house. Exile. Reject.
Abandoned by your husband, you embroidered tears
        into linen. The rocks received you
and you ate them, and served *glyko*, and then walked
        up the steep stairs on short legs.
Yiayia, we swallow stones fragrant with oregano,
        yellow tear stones we pluck from the sea.
Stones make walls but the walls cannot hold back
        the flood. In your kitchen, I hang an icon
of Christ reaching down to pull Adam and Eve
        out of Hell. *Yiayia*, I came to rescue you,
illiterate lady with a steel plate in her head,
        who loved Shirley Temple movies,
who was forced to cook for occupying Nazis,
        who died alone on my birthday while
I crayoned pictures of you in Newburgh, New York.

LIPSTICK

My mother draws a mouth, red and shiny, smoothes it
        over with her pinky, wipes flecks of lipstick from her
teeth, powders her lips white like Greek cookies,
        blots, licks her lips a luscious, lively red,
an illusionist waving a gold wand from Elizabeth Arden,
        rhinestone-tipped magic to transform Monday
into Carnival. Hand-in-hand, we walk to the movies on a summer
        afternoon. In the dark, popcorn and chocolate kisses.
On the screen in black and white, my mother's red lips.

Cousin Christine piles high her hennaed pompadour,
        purples her lips higher than her mouth, wielding
gilt-tubed glamour. Wicked skinny hot lips with a fur stole
        to match, she poses for a glossy picture. In New York
she meets a man who says he'll put her in *Vogue*.
        Seated at the dressing table topped with blue glass and
silver comb and brush, she leans towards me, rubs color
        on my lips with warm, practiced fingers.
Heads together, we practice smiling in the mirror.

Eighteen at the college mixer, I hide the red,
        bite my lips a clean and nervous pale,
hoping to look like a girl who spends her days playing
        tennis. Paralysis. How undressed the naked lips.
How seashell pink, vulnerable. Retreating to
        the lady's room, I dig out Fire and Ice,
paint on a face, make a mouth, needing red lips like Dorothy
        needed ruby shoes. Returning, I'm vermilion
in a sea of rose and peach. A red-haired boy asks me to dance.

LUNCHING WITH LOLA

Just when frivolity's demanded,
      witty repartee glistening with well-voweled,
lipsticked words, why do I want to weep into
      the soup? Lunch out makes me solemn,
this early-century ritual, hot breathy metaphor
      for life, with its beginning, middle and
end, all set on a tiny stage, and
      I play queen to queen, lunching with Lola.

We crack the scripts. Lola breaks the ice.
      I've this yearning in me, I cry,
for white gloves and Cuban heels and love.
      At midday, beef stew fills me with despair.
Lola's laughter splinters glass. That's not it,
      says she, throwing her head back to deposit an
olive pit on my plate. Keep *that* in mind,
      the detritus of betrayal, your ex-husband's
remarriage, sneakered feet and Plath.
      I toss a roll and it bounces off her
forehead. Ooooch, says Lola, unamused.
      So many things happening and not,
connections barely made over the menu
      which wears maroon tassels, like a graduation cap
or a chorus girl's bra. Rolling under the table,
      I drape cloth over my head until
a waiter pulls me out by my feet, careful not
      to snag nylons. Seated again, transfused
with ice water and potage du jour, I read portents
      in the bread basket, observe spies at
the next table. Vanilla ice cream, I shout, its
      truth. Classic as the Parthenon. A bearded
ventriloquist attaches strings to my arms
      and moves them up and down. Did I speak

wrong? There's something on your chin, Lola says.
      The fish arrives without a head.

I bend to kiss Lola's upper hand but she
      retracts it. I squirm and twirl
and swirl and bite. We pat our lips with cloth
      and touch our faces. Lola urges
chocolate mousse and forks me. Blood trickles.
      She'll pay. Next time I treat.

PRISONER OF SUMMER

Through the shutter slits I survey the world like a captive,
      my view narrow, or am I the enemy, aiming fire?
Still, they find me here, view me through the cracks,
      braless, breasts drooping, alone in a blue-green dream,
listening to bird song, church bells, and Stavros next
      door, banging pans, celebrating sorrow.

Aegean prison island where every day I close the
      bars on myself. Clotheslines snap. Cats
take in wash. Birds scream in the heat of twilight.
      Oven world. Inferno of Lemnos. Tonight
trees etch themselves into a Japanese print,
      reminding one of worlds outside.

I come alone, no longer dreaming in the dark
      night that primal dream of men singing in the
square. Now the curtain falls. The
      barbarians are coming with their cement
mixers and computers to repopulate. But I? I never
      belonged, visiting only the house, weeping

in a white plastic chair, remembering my father and
      his pet lamb, slaughtered for an Easter
feast, an early lesson in love. Carefully, I speak to
      everyone, am polite, fear Athena or hope to
meet her in the old lady with her stick, her three
      questions, her pail, her witch's broom.

Island of exile, of remoteness, of widows,
      of misfits, of schemers, of elders
whose hearts burst with goodness. But the whispers,
      the night talk as I'm leaving and black eyes are on me.
The land of green figs and anxiety, of nervous breakdown,
      and yet, and yet, the love.

E. D. KARAMPETSOS

E. D. Karampetsos, PhD in Comparative Literature, the City University of New York Graduate School (1978), teaches in the English Department of the College of Southern Nevada. He has taught at The Bourguiba Institute of the University of Tunis; Deree College in Athens, Greece; Birzeit University in the West Bank, King Faisal University in Saudi Arabia, and Kuwait University. He has published short fiction and articles about contemporary drama and modern Greek culture and literature in: *The Hellenic Journal, Pilgrimage, Coffeehouse, Greek Accent, Grammata ke tehnes, Film Quarterly, World Literature Today, The Journal of Evolutionary Psychology, The Journal of Modern Greek Studies, Abhath Al-Yarmouk, Comparative Literature Studies, The Literary Half-Yearly, Forkroads, Dialogue and Reason, The Looking Glass, The Journal of the Hellenic Diaspora, The Red Rock Review, Mondo Greco, Post-Postmodern Review, Odyssey, Greece in Print,* and *The Charioteer.* He has co-edited a translation, adaptation, and introduction to the seventeenth-century Greek play *The Sacrifice of Abraham,* which appeared at Lycabettos Press (Athens, Greece) in 1989. His book on modern European drama, *The Theater of Healing*, published by Peter Lang, appeared in 1995. He co-authored "The Greeks," a chapter in the anthology *Peoples of Las Vegas: One City, Many Faces* (2005). Pella Press will be publishing his *On the Way to Ithaca,* a collection of essays and articles, and Somerset Hall Press will be bringing out his *Dante and Byzantium.*

WAITING

kneeling
in every nook and cranny
the blossoms cry for light
against the wall a mortal explosion

the planet turns
the shadow
knife of the night
proceeds steadily
the sky is diminished
it cannot contain the flight of a butterfly

SYNTAGMA 1967

Diogenes will not arrive
he was killed near Delphi

there on the right . . .

where is that green fellow running
some car will cut him off in the noise zone
which keeps us here and torments our ears
let him get off that platform
and set aside his ambition
after a coffee he'll recover
his color will return

the other one across the way
died unjustly
they say he demanded freedom or death
let the guard watch him
he's dead after all—he died didn't he

have another coffee
if Diogenes isn't coming
it's possible someone . . . else will bring the light

AT THE REICHENBERGER GRIECHENBEISL

tomorrow I'm going away
I won't be here for the vassilopita
here below the triumphant walls
here where no Ephialtes appears
now with the peace
they have set aside a corner for the cathedral
of Austria Switzerland and Italy
empty titles
the doorman is Austrian

tomorrow I'm going away
I won't be here for the vassilopita
I'm drinking wine and eating a steak
fried with little onions grapes and mushrooms

who cares
the victory was theirs
where will we find ours

Famous for its Viennese food, the Reichenberger Griechenbeisl (or Greeks' Inn) dates back to the sixteenth century. It got its name because it is an area where Greek and Levantine traders settled when trade with the Orient was flourishing. The walls of Vienna stopped the Ottoman advance in Europe. Greeks living in Vienna aided the city's defense and helped repulse two Turkish attacks on the weakened walls at this point. It is next to the Greek Orthodox Holy Trinity Cathedral. Here expatriate Greeks prepared for the revolution of 1821 that led to the liberation of the Greeks and the establishment of the modern Greek state.

THE LAST MONTHS

You have become a dream
a thousand memories of you tremble in my spirit
the precipitation of a distant galaxy
illumines the night of my solitude

the fugitive shadow of a bird in mid-flight
grazes against the walls of my spirit

I know that you exist
I have tasted your lips
the freshness after the rain
I have drowned myself in your eyes
the moon as orange as the blood of clementines
I waited for you to say "I love you"
the caress of Mediterranean waves

ELVIRA'S LESSON

the hysterical voice slices the quiet
into a thousand bloody pieces
the sun flares up and blinds the eyes
red yellow explosion
and the night and the sound
which roars like a savage saw
boring quotations
dyed hair
and the precious hour passes
in mindless waste

the barking of a dog
the flight of a swallow
the cold air of autumn
the sound of leaves falling to the ground
the Chinese vases
                        are drowned out

the veil of chaos
does not conceal   does not explain   does not lie
simplifies everything

HELEN DENDRINOU KOLIAS

Helen Dendrinou Kolias spent her childhood on the island of Cephalonia (where she was born) and in Palaio Phalero, a seaside suburb of Athens. She emigrated to the US with her family at the age of twelve. She is a graduate of Wayne State University (with a BA in Liberal Arts and a major in English) and State University of New York, Binghamton (with an MA and a PhD in Comparative Literature and a Certificate in Literary Translation). She is currently a Visiting Scholar in the Department of Classics at Cornell University, where she has taught Modern Greek and Classics courses for many years, and a Research Associate in the Center for Research and Instruction in Translation at State University of New York, Binghamton, where she has also taught in the Department of English and the Department of Classical and Near Eastern Studies. She is the editor of *Readings in Modern Greek Literature for Intermediate and Advanced Students of Modern Greek* and the translator of numerous selections from Modern Greek poetry and prose into English, including Elisavet Moutzan Martinengou's autobiographical text (*My Story*) and Rhea Galanaki's *I Shall Sign as Loui*.

ΙΕΡΗ ΕΛΙΑ

As I looked out of the crowded bus
I saw the sign for the bus stop.
It read, "Ιερή Ελιά."
I looked in vain
for there was no ελιά
hardly any trees to be seen
along Ιερά Οδός—
only run-down cement blocks
dust and dirt everywhere.

On the road that still leads
to Eleusis
there is nothing sacred
any more
only crammed buses
overloaded trucks
irritated drivers
and weary passengers
trudging along
on what has become
a dreadful road to drive on
in the heart of Athens.

No sign for Eleusis anywhere.
Hardly anyone goes that far.

PASTA FLORA

Among the various gifts
I brought back home
from my last sojourn
in the land of memories
hers stand unique.

Too old to venture beyond her gate
she carries her wobbly frame with difficulty
but finds ways to compensate.

Her gifts are the work of her hands wrapped in love:
knitted socks to warm winter days
a jar of golden jam for morning toast
and a huge pan of *pasta flora*
cut in squares and neatly packed
for the long journey across the Atlantic
intended for loved ones on the distant shore.

As an afterthought, she'd opened a drawer
pulled out a towel of Irish linen
and handed it to me.
"To remember me," she said.

BARBA KOSTAS

We met him the day we arrived in Detroit
—a short and quiet man
his Greek slow and labored
for lack of practice.
He hailed from Constantinople, he said,
rented the house next door—in back
with his Polish wife
and her grown-up daughter.

We often crossed paths
as we came and went
on the sidewalks of our street
—a full head of white hair
his most distinguishing feature.
His words were few but not indifferent.

One day we heard he was diagnosed with cancer
and his face became disfigured.

When he died, the wife
asked me to write a letter
to his relatives in Greece
to let them know.

In the twilight of day
I sat at their kitchen table
transposing formal English tones
into Greek appropriate
for those in mourning.

SOFIA KONTOGEORGE KOSTOS

Sofia Kontogeorge Kostos's heritage is best illustrated by an event that occurred years ago, in her parents' village, Direvmata, on the island of Evvia. As Kostos walked down a dirt road, an elderly woman carrying a pail of fresh figs stopped and offered her a handful, asking, "Whose are you?" Kostos told the woman both of her parents' names. The woman did not recall Kostos's father, because he had left the village to study in Paris, but she remembered her mother. The woman's voice soared with open delight as she exclaimed to her, "Your mother's sewing sang throughout all the villages!"

Kostos is an award-winning photographer and sculptor. She has been writing poems since she was a young girl. She studied the principles of poetry writing with poets Elaine Terranova and Kelly McQuain. Kostos is an advocate for awareness of the Genocides of the Greeks, Armenians, and Assyrians. Her Web site, *Before the Silence,* consists of archival newspaper reports transmitted before 1923, which she researches and transcribes on an ongoing basis. It is hosted by the Armenian Studies Department of the University of Michigan. Thirteen of her poems were included in the *Forgotten Genocides of the 20th Century: A Compilation of Poetry,* edited by Ara Sarafian, the noted historian and editor. Kostos lives in Philadelphia.

A FORTUNE TOLD

Her sunny windowsills were lined
with three dusty alley cats—
guardians of secrets and fortunes
floating in Madam Annie's store-front
salon. Clasping the right palm
of the young woman whose belly

was bursting full of life, Madam
Annie flashed her glistening gold
front teeth. Smiling slowly
and with a deep-accented voice, she said,
"You will have a baby boy."

For emphasis, she added, "Someday
he will be a prince."
Did the Gypsy know
she held my fate in her cupped hand
as Mother gladly placed two silver
coins inside her waiting palm?

I owe my life to the gypsy,
for if she had predicted, "baby girl"
or "princess,"
I would have been a fetus on the bathroom floor.

LITANY OF TEARS

Those who were not burned, drowned themselves

Those who did not drown, were maimed

Those who were not maimed, were stabbed

Those who were not stabbed, starved

Those who were not starved, thirsted

Those who did not thirst, were robbed

Those who were not robbed, were tortured

Those who were not tortured, were hanged

Those who were not hanged, froze

Those who did not freeze, were raped

Those who were raped, went mad

Men, women, children—all

From 1894 to 1922, the Turks proceeded with a "Turkey for the Turks" campaign by systematically torturing and exterminating the original Christian inhabitants of Asia Minor. The exterminations were carried out without bullets. Today, Turkey boasts that its population is homogeneous and 99 percent Muslim.

from *Forgotten Genocides of the 20th Century: A Compilation of Poetry*

DEAN KOSTOS

Dean Kostos is the author of *Last Supper of the Senses* (Spuyten Duyvil, 2005), *The Sentence That Ends with a Comma* (Painted Leaf, 1999), and the chapbook *Celestial Rust* (Red Dust, 1994). He co-edited the anthology *Mama's Boy: Gay Men Write About Their Mothers*, a Lambda Book Award finalist. His poems have appeared in *Barrow Street, The Bitter Oleander, Bloom, Boulevard, Chelsea, Cimarron Review, The Cincinnati Review, Confrontation, Rattapallax, Southwest Review, Stand, Western Humanities Review*, on Oprah Winfrey's Web site *Oxygen.com*, and elsewhere. His reviews have appeared on the Harvard University Press Web site, in *American Book Review*, and elsewhere. His translations from modern Greek have appeared in *Talisman* and *Barrow Street*, and from Spanish (with Jaime Manrique) in *Bomb*. He was commissioned to write *Dialogue: Angel of Peace, Angel of War*, set to music by James Bassi, and performed by Voices of Ascension. *Box-Triptych*, his choreo-poem, was staged at La Mama. He has taught poetry writing at the Gallatin School of New York University, The Columbia Scholastic Press Association, Gotham Writers' Workshop, The Great Lakes Colleges Association, Pratt University, and Teachers & Writers Collaborative. He holds a double MA from Antioch University. Recipient of a Yaddo fellowship, he has served as literary judge for Columbia University's Gold Crown and Gold Circle Awards. He lives in New York City.

INTRODUCING JOHN L. SULLIVAN
a painting by George Bellows

What no one seems to notice is the way
the tuxedo'd announcer's jaw is a cup
from which he pours confidence into himself.
His grayed whiteness tapers into the sheen
of his lapel as another man noses
his face into his ear. This second man
tilts his own thigh slightly, with the lilting
kick of a showgirl, as if in offering.

What no one might want to notice is the referee's
gesture—something like a sneeze, the last
gasp of someone shot in the back,
or the raised hand of a *heldentenor*
shifting from recitative to aria. Even his mouth
is open—not to speak, but to sing
in words whose every vowel is "ah."
What the referee, in the tentativeness of his gesture,

pretends not to notice is the promoter,
who looks as though his head could lift off
from his shoulders like the lid from a teapot—
a ceramic man, the fold in his suit, his collar
and lapel are glazed onto him. The hat
he's holding is an open mouth
to swallow the song, if indeed it is a song,
or only the yawp of the man beside him.

What everyone must notice is the seated boxer
—his swelling calves and sweating biceps—Mr. Sullivan
sitting in the champ's corner of the ring.
Tousled bangs shade deep-set eyes. Or are they

black and blue? He thanks a man (bent in half
like a maître d') who's handing him something.
Or is he taking it away? The two hands merge in one
continuous form like a scroll of paper unrolling.

What everyone might want to ignore
is the bald man: Sullivan's trainer.
His hand curves over the boxer's pale
shoulder, his shaded face breathing words
into Sullivan's ear. Does the trainer want
to caress the boxer? Whatever he
wants, he finds intimacy in being useful
and accepts this role.

What no one notices is the nothingness hung
above the ring like an iron fist, the color
of annealed metal cooling, now cold.
This quadrant of darkness rises
above the referee, above the promoter,
above the trainer, even above Sullivan himself,
casting a stain over the clutter of crowd below,
over you and me, seated there in the second row.

from *Western Humanities Review*

BARBARA LEKATSAS

Barbara Lekatsas is a New Yorker born on the island of Cephalonia. She is the author of *Persephone* (Cross-Cultural Communications Press, 1986) and has been anthologized in *International Women Poets*, edited by Laura Boss (Montclair, New Jersey: LIPS Journal, 1993) and *American Women Poets*, edited and translated into Turkish by Talat Sait Hallman (Varlik Yayinlari, 1992). She has been translated into Greek by Greek poets Katerina Anghelaki-Rooke and Makis Tzilianos. In 1994, she was honored by the Hellenic Heritage and Culture Month committee with commendations from The Council of the City of New York, the Executive Chamber of the State of New York, and the Comptroller of the City of New York for her contribution "to the dissemination of Greek culture and ideals" and also received the Kallistrateon Award for the "perpetuation of Hellenic Culture and History." She is also twice-recipient of a Fulbright Independent Research Grant to Greece and did her doctoral research on Greek Surrealism. She met regularly with Odysseus Elytis, Nikos Engonopoulos, and other Greek writers influenced by the movement and was befriended by the noted translator Kimon Friar. She received her PhD in Comparative Literature from New York University in 1985. She was the first poet featured in the famous poetry readings at Cornelia Street Café. She is a professor of Comparative Literature at Hofstra University and author of scholarly works on the avant-garde and surrealism.

HADES

He confided to her as he trimmed his beard that he himself, at first, didn't like it here. He had grown in the upper regions, had breathed the same ambrosial air as she. He had no taste for the damp. So he became a fire-builder and let the dead ascend to warm themselves slightly above the flame before they were converted into breath for the newly born. He became a builder of tunnels, roads, and cities—a patron of domestic arts and a religious man—insisting on the proper rights of the dead, all accounting neatly done, the interest paid, the memory installed in stone, carved in the native tongue. He was somewhat like her father and expected the traditional things: the cooking, table service, and the dishes done. He became upset around a mess and liked women's work to be done by women. He hardly ate, mistrusted meat, preferring vegetables and bulbs to eat, a little wine to drink, and condiments and sweets. He had the ways of the very old but was wiry and fit when he made love, though impatient and abrupt, conjuring images of women he'd had before and the exploits of love. "A man's a man in heaven or hell," he laughingly said, and seduced her with various intoxicants, then made her dress in the skin of the women that he loved in his dreams.

from *Persephone*, Women Writers Chapbook, Series Editor Stanley H. Barkan (Cross-Cultural Communications, 1986). Copyright © 1986 by Cross-Cultural Communications. Reprinted by permission of the publisher.

THE MEMORY TREE

Black is the color of my love's hair
And black his sloe-shaped eyes
Black is his skin and black his moods
Laconic his replies

Black is the sea on which he sleeps
A boat his trundle bed
Nets neatly spooled his pillows
Dreams folded in his head

Black is the shade of the memory tree
On which I leaned to rest
To cool down from burning thoughts
A handkerchief to fan myself
With which to bid adieu
As his sail dipped beneath the waves
And disappeared from view

Black is the pen
With which I sketch
His reed-like body's stretch
As he casts the nets that bound me
And pulled me to his breast
And black the seas that separate ways
eventually suggest

I placed an orchid by his picture
The photo seemed to laugh
As out of the orchid's petals
Voices whispered "black, black, black."

WHEN I WAS SMALL

When I was small
I recall
I could see Archangels
They were tall, serious, and blonde with curls
Neither man nor woman
But something between boy and girl
And draped in shadowy light.

When I was small
I spoke in Greek:
    Α Γ Γ Ε Λ Ο Σ
    Α
       Ρ
          Χ
             Α
                Γ
                Γ
                   Ε
                      Λ
                        Ο
                          Σ
   Θ Α Ν Α Τ Ο Σ
   Θ
      Ε
        Ο
          Σ
Α Θ Α Ν Α Τ Ο Σ
            Σ
         Ω
      Φ

Winged creatures
Gazing upward in a dome:
Gabriel, Michael
Trumpet and spear
Draped in Greek gear
Gathering souls.

When I was small
My favorite boy
Stuck mud up my hole
And I saw a dead man's bones in the pit of the grave
Gold teeth showing, little moles.

And I ran in a circle
And I ran in an arc
And I said to my grandma,
"Will they do that to you?"
And I said to my mother,
"Why are oranges round?"
And neither could say why one or the other occurred.

When I was small
Earthquakes destroyed our home
I left it all:
The words,
The trees,
The sea,
And flew to another shore
Where angels perched pale as dawn on tombstones
And I went to school
With a head full of curls
And followed the rules
And followed the boys and the girls going to lunch
But at the corner
The light turned green,

The hand went up,
The whistle blew,
And off they flew in every direction
And I sat on the ground
And bitterly cried
Because I didn't know
Which way was home,
When I was small.

from *Persephone*, Women Writers Chapbook, Series Editor Stanley H. Barkan (Cross-Cultural Communications, 1986). Copyright © 1986 by Cross-Cultural Communications. Reprinted by permission of the publisher.

DEMETER IN THE DEEP NORTH

When I set out on my journey,
I packed no provisions for the road.
Like the pilgrim of old,
I simply went with mad abandon,
Convinced I would find my true way.

I set out suddenly,
Abandoning the house:
Better to seek the company of the solitary tree.
A Pain sat beside me
—we were sinking absent-mindedly
into old age.
Occasionally she would drop a phrase,
"Your fault," stare, wait, turn to stone.

I fled while this heavy apparition seemed to sleep.
And then I went into a swoon,
Mindless under a midnight moon,
A sister to the fig leaf.

One morning I found a babe.
We clung together, the child grew strong.
But out of nowhere his parents appeared.
News finally came.
My daughter was married in the South and would return,
In time for the harvest
And in time to give birth.

I built a home in the mountains
To await her every year
My little green kernel
Of joy and despair.

Nostrils full of dust
Tendrils to draw her in
A daffodil.

Dusk upon his fingers
Wind upon his feet
A man in love.

Once corn
Now husk
Dusk falls and falls
Who will lull my baby to sleep?

JOHN MANESIS

John Manesis, a retired physician, and his wife, Bess, have lived in Fargo, North Dakota since 1974. They have four grown children. His poetry has appeared in over twenty publications, including *Wisconsin Review, California State Poetry Quarterly, Zone 3*, and *Footwork: Paterson Literary Review*. His first book of poetry, entitled *With All My Breath*, was published by Cosmos Publishing Company in 2003.

THE ISLANDER'S AUTOPSY

after Elytis

Renowned for its intensity,
Ionian light, the blue and white
enisled within his eye,
illuminates the retina.

A tuft of chamomile
is anchored on his tongue
and scents of basil and oregano
arise from deep within the lungs.

A maroon hue
suffuses his fingertips,
the blush which they absorbed
caressing breasts in many ports.

In the seashell of his inner ear,
one can hear a bouzouki's lament,
the clicking of castanets
and the rustle of a beaded skirt.

Cerebrospinal fluid
that bathes his brain
contains traces of plankton
which have washed ashore.

A garland of anemones
encircles the pericardium
and from an ancient olive tree
a thorn's imbedded in his heart.

KATHRYN MARIS

Kathryn Maris was born in New York and educated at Columbia University and Boston University. She has held two poetry fellowships at the Fine Arts Work Center in Provincetown and residencies at Yaddo and the Ragdale Foundation. Her poems have appeared in magazines such as *American Poet*, *Fence*, *Ploughshare*s, and *Poetry*, and in *New Voices: University and College Prizes*, an anthology edited by Heather McHugh. In addition, she regularly contributes essays and book reviews for *Poetry London* magazine. A lecturer in Creative Writing at Morley College in south London, she divides her time between London and New York City. Her collection, *The Book of Jobs*, was released from Four Way Books in autumn of 2006.

GODDESS

I love a bare world, like the world I strode with my boy.
I held his hand. I said, "This is a *wall* of wind." I flung

the words over the wall, but the wind-whirr deafened him.
His walk was a wrestle. The wan sky was his twin.

His father beckoned him to the swings
and the world grew barer. My son's love is a burden,

the Oedipal beat, beat, beat of his fist on his
father's tee-shirted chest. I see

that his leaving will repeat itself, and I will let him leave.
And I love a bare world.

Once my husband declared me a goddess
of destruction. I approved of that view. I view

myself that way, too: Queen of an Uninhabited Planet.
I tread on moon-rubble. Dust circles my knees.

My dress is Belgian deconstructionist. I am barefoot and regal
and unadorned but for the bracelet from the ward.

I am mother to all that is bare, all that is gone
for I have expected the bare world all along.

From *Poetry London*

HANSEL IN THE CAGE

> *My father bars the door, bars harm*
> *From this house, and it is years.*
> —Louise Glück, "Gretel in Darkness"

I was fearless under the firmament,
the starry dark
my first education in freedom.

It was my last. On the second night—
when there were no guiding stones—
it was clear:

The expanse was a cold globe
and we were its prisoners.
I saw the world strangely—

I saw prisons in everything.

Now I sit in one:
bone bars and a lonely triumvirate
of me, my wits, and a chicken bone.

As I fatten, I watch the sugar-glazed window.
What is a tree that lives in a sea of trees
if not a prisoner?

Trees: my father's ruin.
His wife: his ruin. Hunger: our ruin.
Our bodies: our ruins.

If there is ever escape, may it be ecstatic.
If there is glass to be shattered as in a snowglobe
let me shatter the sky and live without it.

from *Ploughshares*

OPHTHALMOLOGY AT DAWN

Dawn is ugly, a fug over day,
a tarpaulin
on a top-of-the-line motorcycle.

An amaryllis
has a hideous nativity:
two shoots peer from the bulb

frantically as a chick
peers out of its ovular jail.
Beginnings are rarely pretty:

think of sperm, woolly
mammoths, pre-atmospheric
goo. Beginning, too,

is the hardest part of work,
so dawn is another affront
like taxes, insurance or rent.

Still, the amaryllis that erupts
so horrifically from its bulb
does eventually unfold

a dazzling, two-headed
megaphone.
And in the machinery

of ophthalmology
the retina is a forest at dusk
reddening beneath the beaming

optic disc. The eye
is diachronic because it sees
the past in everything

and because it's a planet
with a setting sun
no matter the time of day.

from *Ploughshares*, subsequently on *Poetry Daily*

THE END OF ENVY

The end of envy
Is a staircase in midair.

From there,
There is nothing to want,

But there is wind to love.
I miss what the wind bent,

But I'm used to the bare world.

When I was sentenced to the stairs
For eternity, I didn't know

I would climb them pregnant,
Or ill, or with the aim of soothing a cry

That would reappear
As soon as I was at the bottom.

In a way I am happy here on the stairs,
For the end of envy

Is the end of desire, the end of the edifice,
But not of elevation.

from *Ploughshares*

THE BOATMAN

Ruddy rower of the boat called Merry Man, merry
man of the dark marsh, host of the party barge.

His arms are like a farmer's: slight but hard
from the drag and the drag of a task—

the oars that lap the flat of the black bog
until the reedmace sways its kinky heads.

I see the boat from the land where I stand.
I can see the greasy distance, and the boatman's grin.

He likes his drink. His myopia is a droll trick.
When he snakes into the far-off, his focus goes vague

and he's known to mistake a quarrel for a dance,
an embrace for containment, ardor for arduousness.

I am the same. I see what I want when he is far,
when love goes distant. I can see him and then I can't

and then I can and, when I can, I see the merry man,
the merry man is really just the ferryman.

from *Poetry London*

THANASIS MASKALERIS

Thanasis Maskaleris was born in Arkadia, Greece and immigrated to the US at the age of 17. He studied Philosophy and English at the University of Oklahoma, and Comparative Literature at Indiana University and UC Berkeley. He has written original poetry in Greek and in English, and has translated contemporary Greek poetry and prose extensively.

Maskaleris has taught Classics, Comparative Literature, and Creative Writing at San Francisco State University, until his recent retirement. He has also been Director of the Center for Modern Greek Studies since it was founded in 1981 (until 1996) and has coordinated efforts that led to the establishment of the Nikos Kazantzakis Chair at SFSU. He has recently co-translated, into English, Nikos Kazantzakis's *Russia*, and is currently working on a critical biographical study of Kazantzakis.

During the past 20 years he has frequently served on the Executive Committee of the Modern Greek Studies Association. His most recent publication (co-edited with Nanos Valaoritis) is *Modern Greek Poetry: An Anthology* (Talisman House Publishers, 2004).

SUN MOON LAKE

for Mina

There is no sun here. No moon.
Only you, and this gentle lake . . .

I look at you on our new bed,
your eyes eclipsed in your moon-sent crimson sleep.
And I, a waning sun, watching the cloud-brimmed peaks
thinking of the poets of China,
ghosts now in the landscapes they loved.

You and I in this emptied heaven,
pulled together by our own sun and moon.

UNNATURAL TUMBLEWEEDS

On this barren slope, incessantly besieged by winds,
I used to race the bouncing tumbleweeds down to the pebbled shore;
or, lying at the water's edge, I would wait for them to descend
and then, with a soccer-trained kick, I would send them
into the sea, toward new, wave-tossed journeys . . .

Beyond this rugged hill, across Persephone's meadow,
they would gather their shadow-growing bodies
and roll on unchartered paths.

Here, on this sacred field, I first spun my growing dreams.

And now, in this troubled Spring, on the same Aegean shore,
I turn my back to the once magic slope,
trying to block off, as in a nightmare, the new tumbleweeds—
plastic bags, billowing in the wind, descending on the littered shore.

How long before Persephone returns to bring her green spring
to our choking earth?

ANDRIANA MASTOR

Andriana Mastor's connection to Greece traces back to her grandparents, who emigrated to the United States in the postwar wave of the 1920s. She studied English literature at UC Berkeley. She received her MA from UCLA in Comparative Literature, with a focus on ancient Chinese literature of the Tang and Song Dynasties. She is currently working on her PhD in Comparative Literature at UCLA. Her main areas of focus are contemporary American poetry and ancient Greek epic and lyric poetry. She studies contemporary poetry with Stephen Yenser, in particular the work of James Merrill. She has been active in the contemporary poetry scene in New York and in San Francisco, where she organized poetry readings for Intersection for the Arts and participated in Poet's Theater. Her own poetry is inspired by various sources, including Chinese and Japanese lyric as well as the poetry of ancient and modern Greece; she is currently working on a translation of Yannis Ritsos's *Helen*. For Mastor, poetry is a sympathy of thought between worlds, languages, points in time, or people, and her love for Greece is a bridge she frequently travels. She lives in New York.

GREEK LESSONS

> φεύγω για τα ξένα, για την ξενιτιά
> και μην κλαις για μένα, αγάπη μου γλυκιά
> —Μίκης Θεοδωράκης
> I'm leaving for faraway lands, for distant lands
> and don't weep for me, my sweet love
> — Mikis Theodorakis

Sweetgrowing basil and purple hyacinth
mingle on a ledge a few steps from the sea
and she honeyvoiced sings to me, a song she
tries to teach me and

points to the tiny leaves to show me a word,
basilikós, the fragrance lingers on our
tongue, the moonlight on our table, rakes a
heart which fiercely proud

of long roots in rich, dry soil cradles sounds new
but felt in dreams as salt in my skin, and I
heave them up stone-shod hills, wait for the mind to
ripen thought like figs

still green in June, yet oleander blossoms
burst over this island in a crimson blush
that stretches to sea to be quenched, or fanned, as
flames meet lap of foam

and nights I lie alone, conjugating you,
conjuring you, my mother's mother's tongue which
love tied me up in with the first syllable,
now blows with the tide

to arms of dawn lit on sea, the bouzouki
player strings his notes, we toss roses up, out,

we walk, linked arm-in-arm, into arms of roses
which usher the dream

and I let you lead me, cradle my small hands,
*kai pame stin alli geitoniá gia na
zitísoume fotiá*—to borrow fire from
a neighbor's village—

and we trace our path between fingers, my small
knuckles are tall mountains, blue mountains of fair
Tríkala, where longing still floats in the eyes of
an old flame of yours,

who drags his hay-heavy mule up a winding
road to the village where once you too lived
and a drop falls for each syllable of you,
my *Aspasía*.

TO LOVE

We have words for love in Greece—
agapi holds the world ajar
and sky and fields easily fit
and clouds of cotton in a jar.

Eros is the mover, though—
an arrow knocked and loosed
wrenches fingers, stretches thumb—
the arrow flies away.

Arrows arc like thoughtless thought
or the sea run to its surf
and suddenly you know you're caught.
(He soaks my heart of earth

and then the salt begins to sting.)
But love, what metal greaves
my beloved's shins, solders his soul,
my broken arrows at his feet?

I love him still—a dream's close
at curl of glass—but still
love can draw no bows. So Eros,
my sweet—melt me a quill.

HOPPER: *ROOMS FOR TOURISTS*

I try on these paintings like rooms.
This one, for example, a seaside
bed & breakfast painted
oilthick white on clapboard,
flanked by mintgreen
shutters that set off yellow light
beautifully, such a light that
holds a secret of warmth
in its smear of glow.
Now take a look inside (go ahead!
Hopper did, night layered upon night,
without even asking the landlady!),
peer into the long window, *there*,
behind the slip of kitchen table—
do you see a coffee-colored cupboard
stacked with eggshell saucers, or
a pair of pitchers, perhaps, and
do you see, behind them, a piece
of white rectangle? And do
you see yourself there, peering
back out at you?

Well not me but then I'm not
really able to reflect on myself
while I'm on this earth, for that matter.
What I want to know is whether
to let love flood into its room
though it may leave me
out on this chill sea street.

So I'm sitting outside
this house with my back to it,
having knocked myself silly
with knocking on doors that
give way like paint. Its yellows
and whites, its bluishgreens
its blackforest awnings,
the lilting shadow of its roof,
these do not hold me as I'm
still a tourist. There *is* no room
for tourists. Why don't I know this
from the start? Why do I sit here,
night layered upon night?

CHERT

You trace your roots
to the ancient sea
sponge, or some other
ocean creature not allowed
a proper burial. Your life
remains within you, compressed,
not as genes but as matter,
your once sponge-self congealed
to its core, tossed in rivers, seas.
The insult spreads.
Your dark fractures
speak of surfaces assaulted by the same
old story, life after life. Some century,
fed up and flinty,
you'll find a hand
to break,
flake you into the head
of an arrow,
fresh-cut for flight.

SLATE

Fine streaks of silky
brown weave into gray-
black matter. You slice
sveltely into sheets
thin as thought.
You crack
and split along planes—
what perfect cleavage!—
but not a favored
trait, by the lights of those
who'd make grave
markers of you. I keep you
for my own means,
admire the way you are
easily rubbed clean.

CLEOPATRA MATHIS

Cleopatra Mathis was born and raised in Ruston, Louisiana. Her first five books of poems were published by Sheep Meadow Press, and are distributed by University Press of New England. *What to Tip the Boatman?* won the Jane Kenyon Award for Outstanding Book of Poems in 2001. A new collection of poems, *White Sea*, was published by Sarabande Books in 2005.

Mathis's work has appeared widely in anthologies, textbooks, magazines and journals, including *The New Yorker, Poetry, American Poetry Review, Tri-Quarterly, The Southern Review, The Georgia Review, The Made Thing: An Anthology of Contemporary Southern Poetry, The Extraordinary Tide: Poetry by American Women*, and *The Practice of Poetry*. Various prizes for her work include two National Endowment for the Arts grants, in 1984 and 2003; the Peter Lavin Award for Younger Poets from the Academy of American Poets; two Pushcart Prizes, 1980 and 2006; The Robert Frost Resident Poet Award; a 1981-82 Fellowship in Poetry at the Fine Arts Work Center in Provincetown, Massachusetts; The May Sarton Award; and Individual Artist Fellowships in Poetry from both the New Hampshire State Council on the Arts and the New Jersey State Arts Council.

Mathis is the Frederick Sessions Beebe Professor of the Art of Writing at Dartmouth College, where she directs the Creative Writing Program. She lives with her family in Hanover, New Hampshire.

LIVING NEXT DOOR TO THE CENTER FOR COLD WEATHER

It's more than you see: Cold Regions
Research Lab protected by its chain-link fence
on this street of pre-fab housing. And behind it,
the blank green knoll I can't get to,
a little field on the crest of the hill
and to the far right, an old cedar
like the one in my great-aunt's kitchen yard.
But the land behind the house
takes a steep dip into a kind of gouge
filled with waist-high scrub and razorweed
rising to a mangy tangle of poplar
that climbs the other side. There's no path
except the line some garbage-seeking skunk
or raccoon has pressed around the hill,

and all those over there are separated from me.
Young again, they speak—the aunts with their crochet
and warnings, my grandfather shaking his thin trees
hard to bring down the rain of olives.
And coughing Theo, whose knee is the first I remember,
the anonymous lifting me up.
                            It is the cough I think
wakes me, the hacking in some faltering machine
that runs all night in the center for cold weather.
Windows and back door tight, it still invades,
sporadic over the whiter noise and hourly
thumping of some monitor for the gravity of cold.

Newcomer at the edge of an imposing winter,
what do I know about freezing, about thaws
of such shade and density they can take years.
I can't imagine a temperature as low as they claim,
weathering as I do these other reminders—

the family gestures, the particular
throw of the hand in the slaughter of lambs.
I see the small flaws in their skin, the mottled
red mole that finally killed one, another's birthmark
like one of Easter's red eggs.
Maybe I've brought them up here to bury
under snow, up there in the serene heart of it,
away from the gray roadside clumps, the plow's
manufactured wall, or the news of pressure systems.

Maybe their presence is no more unlikely than
machines that measure cold and the fracture
thickness of ice. Some mornings I think I'll
put on the right shoes and take some kind of tool
to hack my way up there. Maybe then I'd see
beyond them, down the other side of the hill
to a river. Hills do fall away into rivers
and the Connecticut is nearby.
The water this time of year is low and still,
even warm, and I could lie down in it.
Looking back to this house
next to the industry of weather-keeping,
perhaps I would see not so much the bleak yard, the fifties'
box housing in yellow, pink, and blue,
but some shelter beyond the past.
I'd love this life for what it is,
intact, the simple day by day,
loved for its necessities;
no waking to the dread of what's lost.

Ask me what matters and I'll say
it is the nightmare of this place,
the time of weather change and cover, the hours
made of a small field and one tree
the chilled room of sleep with the recurring
face of my thirty-year-old mother.

Nothing then has changed, yet outside
the drive of machinery
beats with the warp and turn of winter.
I am more a visitor on this street
than one who wakes at home in the center's
order of snow.
                Sleeping to return, I find
the room where I made my first goodbye,
like communion or baptism, to provide
the ritual groundwork of my need.
She took me there to kiss him,
grandfather, his lips
dedicated to what passed between them:
breath and Greek, a tongue almost religious
in rural Louisiana. All night he sang the names
that meant a life to him. All night
the banded wrist rose and hesitated,
marking time with the hand
that would not be still.

Then sometime toward the end
she pushed me to him. There resting on his chest,
with the blue-veined wires, God's picture,
which I refused to kiss even for the dying—
not yet knowing the season that assigns the heart its story.

from *The Center for Cold Weather*

FLOWERS

These blossoms outside the window
have nothing to do with the twentieth century.
Theirs is a foreign story,
more foreign than their name from the East,
since the East draws closer these days,
and their imposing health
belongs to a tree that thrives on its own.
What does the Chinese plum have to do with history,
the great public and private sorrows?
The present looms, assuming and yet
detached, the stems woven for the purposes
of their branches. The tree limits what I can see,
pulling me in to regard my ordered room,
so I cannot know the Vermont pastures
where the vapory rain of isotopes
bonds with the compounds the grass drinks in
and the cows eat. My friend takes iodine,
on the safe side. What thick healthy flowers
distract me, what beauty bars the window
with its exclusive transformation,
not unlike government promises
on this morning of my grandmother's ninetieth birthday.
Seventy years ago, every member of her family
and an entire culture died at the hand of the Turks.
Flowers, she says, belong in the grave,
where they cover the dead,
not the face of what we live.
My grandfather lived in this country
fifty years without learning the language,
yet never went back to Mytilene. He kept himself
surrounded by his gardens, his trees. His roses
meant nothing to her.

from *The Center for Cold Weather*

CLEOPATRA THEODOS

We had language between us: her trick
of pretending not to know English
when she didn't want to speak. I pretended
not to know Greek, and so it went
that way for years, a clear standoff
in which she learned to get what she wanted
by staring deep into my face. The easy
track of my childhood never lied.
Her reward was my affliction: sties
flowered in my eyes. Around the iris
red flamed its way, evil she could see
settling in its rim. She knew some magic words,
province of one firstborn protecting another,
and she gave them, chanting and gesturing,
her face transfixed by mine.
Whatever the devil is, he listened
to her voice. She lured him out
into her atmosphere and pinned him to the meanest year:
to the twenty-four years her first child lived
and the scimitar's blade in her mother's belly,
its few minutes of wrath against hidden children.
Five brothers in a nation of murdered children
came back and spoke, safe for once
in the sanctuary of her face. Held there in Ayvali,
stone's throw from the ancient cities of grief,
the devil met his history. His gift for division
could not stand up to the power of her losses.
Though he would keep coming back with his attempts
to burrow in, to follow the light through the optic nerve
leading to the back of the brain,
to that tiny center where the soul is housed,
no matter how he tried
to fix the fine point of his greed,

she lifted my chin and studied the possibilities:
the little tear ducts beginning to swell,
some threat of cloud in the innocent blue.
Over me, she spoke for heaven. Words opened
her hands and bound me to her.
With that music, with the light of her eyes,
she whipped him, dismissed him, and he fled.

from *The Center for Cold Weather*

THE SOURCE

Morning arrives in Louisiana, green going sour
with heat. Against the screen, oleander
scrapes its thicket of blooms,

cardinals gather in the yard, too many to count
with their rough voices, the single abrupt chirp.
My grandfather will not touch those birds,

though he shoots others with a stone and sling
and stews them whole,
nested in onion broth with whole garlic and clove.

Plain brown wrens, song sparrows—for him
no different from the figs he picks into his hat.
I hide in the Muscadine vines

pretending to play. He can't speak English
and I won't speak Greek. I can hear him calling,
each word hitting its mark,

and so I go to him with all my refusal.
From the blushing spot on each blossom end,
he peels back the skin for the fig's red meat,

he slips the coarse black covers off the grapes
and feeds me in the shade. It's too hot.
I lick the skin on my forearm. He's talking,

telling me that taste is like the sea.
I have never seen the sea. He's in another country
trying to tell me something. I look away.

from *White Sea*, published by Sarabande Books, Inc. © 2005 by Cleopatra Mathis. Reprinted by permission of Sarabande Books and the author.

ZAHARATI MORFESIS

Zaharati Morfesis holds a BFA in Fine Arts from Kutztown University of Pennsylvania and an MA in Liberal Studies from Rutgers University. Zaharati held a Rotary International Ambassadorial Scholarship to Greece to study Goddess mythology, an Andrew W. Mellon Program Grant in art history, and received the Alumni Award from Rutgers University, Camden, for academic achievement. She has worked with youth and adults as an art teacher at Ionian Village, Greece, for *Peace Through the Arts for Cyprus*, as an adjunct in the Department of Fine Arts, Rutgers University, and currently as a writing workshop leader.

Her writings have appeared in the *Journal of Graduate Liberal Studies*, *The National Herald*, *The Hellenic Chronicle*, *The Orthodox Observer*, *The Courier-Post*, *The Philadelphia Inquirer*, and *Poetry Greece*. She has performed at the Walt Whitman Center for the Arts in their *NJ Writers Series* and was a featured presenter at the AHEPA District 5 Hellenic Cultural Celebration for New Jersey and Delaware. Her one-woman show, *Persephone and Hades*, written and performed by Zaharati and directed by Lili Bita, was performed for the Philadelphia Fringe Festival and at Rutgers Camden Center for the Arts.

Zaharati's creative and academic work is inspired by mythology and the notion of transformation, both personal and global.

THE KING

my soul
is filled
with your
scent
warm, layered
hot
mercurial
each
valley is carved
with the trace
of your footsteps
each tree bends
to the whisper of
your hidden names
and when I
dream
you appear
more so
than in
my waking hours
what have I done
to deserve all that
you can't give me
I anoint myself
with holy oil
and invoke
barriers to your
spirit
penetrating
me
yet
we know
the futility

of keeping
my shadow
exiled
impossibilities
are everything
consumed
and infatuated
broken-hearted
and betrayed
I wait
I wish
I wonder
and still you
elude me
everything
is fading
the night sky
covers
the day
I pray
I cease to pray
I am the result
of your countless
blessings
the by-product
of your pain
what cruel and
inhuman
deeds
did I commit
in knowing you

SUBTERRANEAN SKIES

under
subterranean skies
I wander
like a mist
my hair blends
in with the
formless vapors
that surround me
I walk
floating
I sink
in the murky waters
entwined with
roots of trees
pretending to live
faint cries fill the
air
and I move
in their direction
placing my hand
upon their souls
giving them a
moment's healing
yet my hands
can't heal my own
heart
I'm tired
I want my own home
I want to look up
and see a
real sun
shining bright
burning the
subterranean sky
from my sight

NIKKI MOUSTAKI

Nikki Moustaki holds an MA in poetry from New York University and an MFA in the same from Indiana University. She is the author of *The Complete Idiot's Guide to Writing Poetry* (Alpha Books, 2001) and is a recipient of a 2001 National Endowment for the Arts Grant in poetry. Moustaki has taught Creative Writing at New York University, Indiana University, and The New School. Her poetry publication credits include *Quarterly West, Cream City Review, Alaska Quarterly, TriQuarterly, Spoon River Poetry Review, Many Mountains Moving, PIF Magazine, American Literary Review, Yemassee Review, Madison Review, Berkeley Poetry Review, Cimarron Review, Amaranth, Yankee Magazine,* and *Poetry After 9-11: An Anthology of New York Poets,* among others. Her poetry has also appeared in anthologies and college textbooks. She is a fulltime freelance writer with over 30 books to her credit, as well as hundreds of articles in a diverse array of magazines, such as *Jane, Latina, Humanities* (the National Endowment for the Humanities magazine), *Dog Fancy, Bird Talk*, and many others. She lives in New York City and is owned by two dogs and a noisy parrot.

NIGHT PLUMBER

My neighbor comes at one a.m. in her night
clothes to say my toilet's screaming in the pipes
through her walls, and before I can turn her
away or tell her to joggle the handle she's got it
disassembled, got her hands wet, and now I
hear the water too, wasting away in our old
shared pipes, trying to spin some long mystery,
filling and refilling the basin, writing with rust
in perfect lines, wasting while the whole town
sleeps, water incognito; my neighbor yanks
the chain, bobs the rubber stopper, the water
rests at last, my neighbor drags her damp socks
back to bed. This embryonic Tuesday flutters
in its darkness around me like a new moth;
crickets; an ambulance; my steam heat ticking
its own old pipes with some other ancient code—
I try to decipher sleep again, hearing the very air
above my bed scratch its legs against the ceiling,
realizing I was smothered a little every night
by my toilet, of all the ridiculous things, renegade
water, or some tired bit of rubber permitting
the innocent water through, the hushing music,
like a friend saying *don't be lonely*, or *I'm lonely too*.

WRITING POEMS ON ANTIDEPRESSANTS

Writing poems on antidepressants
is hard. You can appreciate the difficulty
by reading the previous two lines.
Metaphors are easy
to come by when you're aching
or pining or wounded in love,
which scientists have proven is a type of madness
and madness can be cured with a pill.
Not every day
is Paris. Not every day
does a bird come winging
out of a carpet to give you a free metaphor,
especially if there are oranges on the table
and you're on your meds.
Each day offers some little irony or a dream
or a blind albino woman
sitting next to you on the train
with eyelashes like white silk threads
attached like broom-straw to her one closed eye
as she taps her cane against the window
and you, the poet on antidepressants,
thinks: look at that, hmmm, interesting.
Did I buy dog food? Here's my stop.

HOW TO WRITE A POEM AFTER SEPTEMBER 11TH

First: don't use the word *souls*. Don't use the word *fire*.
You can use the word *tragic* if you end it with a k.
The rules have changed. The word *building* may precede
The word *fall*, but only in the context of the buildings falling
Before the fall, the season we didn't have in Manhattan
Because the weather refused, the air refused . . .
Don't say the air smelled like smoldering desks and drywall,
Ground gypsum, and something terribly organic,
Don't make a metaphor about the smell, because it wasn't
A smell at all, but the air washed with working souls,
Piling bricks, one by one, spreading mortar.
Don't compare the planes to birds. Please.
Don't call the windows eyes. We know they saw it coming.
We know they didn't blink. Don't say they were sentinels.
Say: we hated them then we loved them then they were gone.
Say: we miss them. Say: there's a gape. Then, say something
About love. It's always good in a poem to mention love.
Say: if a man walks down stairs, somewhere
Another man is walking up. Say: he sits at his desk
And the other stands. He answers the phone and the other
Ends a call with a kiss. So, on a rainy dusk in some other
City of Commerce and Art, a mayor cuts a ribbon
With giant silver scissors. Are you writing this down?
Make the executives parade through the concourse,
Up the elevators to the top, where the restaurant,
Open now for the first time, sets out a dinner buffet.
Press hard. Remember, you're writing with ashes.
Say: the phone didn't work. Say: the bakery was out of cake,
The dogs in the pound howled. Say: the world hadn't
Asked your permission to change. But you were asleep.
If you had only written more poems. If only you had written

More poems about love, about peace, about how abstractions
Become important outside the poem, outside. Then, then,
You could have squinted into the sky on September 11th
And said: thank you, thank you, nothing was broken today.

PITA BREAD

Even in flour Nona's hands are darker than mine—
She's rolling pinched dough into thin disks,
laying them to mature on every flat surface in the house.

Crouching at the oven's window, I watch the circles grow
from alabaster to sand, stretch to the oven's top like inflatable globes.

She was born in Egypt, breadth of flat breads, three world wonders,
a backwards river with an ambiguous source—
the oldest of six, she quit school to raise bread,
sent the stomachs of her siblings full into the world.
In Miami, the pita just doesn't rise the same.

Watching her sacrifice turned delight, I might understand that other oven—
Nona sweating in the Alexandrian heat, young and whole with questions,
full with my father she doesn't know yet, not suspecting American me.

Skimming slim dough through the hot door, each done batch
into brown grocery bags to cool, I'm her, the woman quiet
as to not upset the bread, woman baking, now, to sustain nothing
    but her fancy.
Her click-clacking slippers sucking the voice starting in my throat.

The silence is reverent, the memory of practical hunger,
the yeasty smell of suffering filling the neighbors' houses.

Cleaning bowls with white, sticky hands, I'm also carrying
a country full of questions—I want to know how the pocket
enters the pita, how the pita knows to fill itself with space:

she stops mid-roll, throws more flour on the slab,
and it's all there in her face:
The dough knows what kind of bread to be.
It's the mouth that has to wait.

SELF-PORTRAIT WITH FLOWERS

In this painting there's a boy standing beside me—
once there was a kind of flagpole in the distance
before the boy absorbed it with his own javelin-body and darkened face.

Behind him an empty window bright with kitchen,
silver gleam half-open to the night and the boy is smelling pie—
should it be pie? With his white fingers he cuts a slice.

He doesn't notice me brushing my hair behind him.
Perhaps fifteen years he hasn't tasted this light
through his mother's window, and now he watches
as she moves along the row of shutters,

an opaque pain in his tongue, as if he swallowed
a whole town: one steeple, one museum, one bear in a cage.
I'm asleep in the painting where the boy
takes a half-step toward the mother and she says
look out where you're going.

Seeing him stumble, I imagine the portrait where he doesn't wake up.
She weeps, or I hope she weeps.
I think of her as the kind of painting you'd hang near a piano.

Here we are, the wind calling with a dream and a funeral—
does it matter where I place the flowers?
Things finish without us, even days.

How to live unembarrassed about this?
How to remember that the canvas is always silent
among the other faces, the other positively human things?

Here the mother speaks of these windows made beautiful
despite fading, despite the simplicity of perspective.
She leans from the window, now yellow, now green with dusk.
This is, after all, merely a rib showing through skin,
quite legible. This is my own window.

I know the paint loves me as one loves some confiscated thing,
an eye to a sharpened stick, dullness creeping upon us like a jungle.
Where is the blame in brushing one's hair for the portrait?
Only later I'll remember there's a kind of forgiveness
among turpentines. Then, it's best to go home.

KOSTAS MYRSIADES

Kostas Myrsiades, professor of Comparative Literature and English at West Chester University, is a distinguished translator and Neohellenist and the first American to receive the Gold Medallion (1995) for his translations from the Hellenic Society of Translators of Literature given annually by the Greek government to a scholar from any country. His work in Greek letters is not only demonstrated in his 17 published books and numerous articles on modern and ancient Greek literature but also in the many invited lectures he has delivered for such groups as the Jane Globus Seminar Series Lecture at Baruch College, the Elytis Chair Lecture Series of Poetry and Neohellenic Studies at Rutgers, and the Embassy of Greece/National Library of Canada Lecture at Ottawa. He is the editor of *College Literature*, a quarterly of literary criticism, theory, and pedagogy, which since 1990 has been the recipient of six awards from the Council of Editors of Learned Journals including the Phoenix Award for distinguished editorial achievement. Professor Myrsiades also co-edits the *Journal of the Hellenic Diaspora*, one of the leading journals in Neohellenic studies.

ODYSSEUS AND PENELOPE SECRETLY PLOT AGAINST THE SUITORS

for Linda

> *And may the gods accomplish your desire:*
> *a home, a husband, and harmonious converse*
> *with him—the best thing in the*
> *world being a strong house held in*
> *serenity where man and wife agree. Woe*
> *to their enemies, joy to their friends!*
> *But all this they know best.*
> Odyssey *VI*, Trans. by Richmond Lattimore

True revolutions
are ignited by consenting minds
erupting spontaneously
whenever eye meets eye
as when Penelope before the beggar caught Odysseus' eye.

"Stranger," she said.
"I shall decree a contest on this day.
One arrow must each suitor whip through twelve ax heads;
something only my lord can do."

The beggar relaxed his eyes.

"Let there be no postponement of this trial.
Death to the suitors, lady, not one will escape his doom."

Their gazes touched once again
and both Odysseus and Penelope

knew.

A CENTAUR PREPARES AN EMIGRANT FOR HIS JOURNEY ABROAD

after Pasolini's Medea

"Beyond that black streak on the lucid sea,"
the man-horse said,

"where reason is far different from our own,
reality is myth and only the mythical are real. There you
will recover the golden fleece."

"Beyond the boundary of the sky
where the sun turns black as a horsehair sack,"
the human horse
observed,

"you will find a love
who will ax for you her flesh
to steal the ram's gold hide
that you may learn the goatskin's worth."

"Then in a world that ignores the vineyards for the sea,"

the desecrated beardless horse
explained,

"she will bear you sons
whom she will baptize in blood
and you will raise in flames."

THE EMIGRANT SETS OUT FOR AMERICA
after Seferis

We anchored
below the setting of the sun
past the cape of dogs that howl
seeking the other life beyond the statues.
On the dark side of the sun
we dug our votive pit
and there gushed the murky blood from slashed and bleating
ewes.

                                    Slowly,
                        slowly they came,

thin and thirsty forms
to drink of the somber blood,
but we kept from the gurgling pit the driving apparitions
until the old man's faint image bent toward the blood and
spoke,

       "Anguish lies ahead on the godly sea."

THE HOUSE IN VOURLIOTES

The saints in their wooden casings
looked stern above the stained bed sheets
(which smelled of urine)
next to the asbestos-white fireplace.

Only the droning of the rain
beat on the wood window shutters
and on the tine awning of the outer door.

On the village square,
iconic figures sipped ouzo
and eyeballed a young blond tourist
who crossed her legs
to expose a dozen fleshy thighs.

From the cafés
a siren beckoned
with the smell of resin wine
and the beguiling sounds
of bubbling narghiles.

STEPHANOS PAPADOPOULOS

Stephanos Papadopoulos was born in 1976, raised in Paris and Athens and holds a degree in classical archaeology from the University of North Carolina at Chapel Hill. His work has appeared in periodicals such as *The Yale Review, Poetry Review, The New Republic,* and many others. His poetry has been translated into Greek by the acclaimed poet Katerina Anghelaki-Rooke, as well as selections into Spanish, French, and Italian. He has translated works of the Greek poets Yiannis Ritsos, Anghelaki-Rooke, and Kostas Karyotakis. He has edited and co-translated the Selected Poems of Derek Walcott for Kastaniotis Press in Greece. *Lost Days*, his first collection, is published by Michael Hulse with Leviathan Press in London and Rattapallax Press in New York. His second book, *Casual as Birds*, is forthcoming.

AN INHERITED MEMORY OF WAR

My great grandfather rides a white horse,
travels the Black Sea fields clip-clopping
the dusty roads from which the hardest
rain will run like blood into the stubble.
He wears black in the merciless sun,
sells tobacco, counting crops and profits
from a green leaf held to the light.
He knows with animal conviction
that steel burns white as the sickle moon,
that it takes a generation of dead
to raise another. He crosses himself,
lays a palm across his heart,
stands stone-faced in the smoky church
while the priest swings his blazing censer.
There are times in the insomniac dark
while his wife and children lie sleeping
that he doubts God, has a vision
of black angels and muskets rearing,
his home a rising cumulus of smoke
as the boys traverse the trampled rows
of the fading crop unpicked and curling,
and he hears a pop when young Aristotle
falls short of the fence, holds his chest and bleeds
into his father's field, plants his bones.

MAVRAKI

I

In the burnt yellow afternoon light of Kouzi,
Mavraki sits with the old men—
leather boots left to dry in the sun.
Wars move quickly, then there is the memory.
The sun moves across the pockmarked wall where
rust stains lead down from railings,
the tear marks of iron eighty years exposed.
The building stands like a sick horse;
walls crumble when touched, crippled foundations
turned to limestone dust, and the memory of plumbing
risen to the surface like veins.
Mavraki pushes his cart through streets that sigh
with too much history, an old man
trying to forget a memory packed with salt.

II

Mavraki passes churches, crossing himself (in case)
while shopkeepers stand like question marks in doorways,
as he traces the snail's path through sidewalks
that speak of old Athens through forty-year cracks,
of a younger, lighter man.
In Papandreou's tavern, he swallows the last strings of tripe,
a glass of wine, smokes cigarettes and waits.
Everyone waits,
as mosquitoes die tiny deaths on light strips
and the accordion shudders, gasping.
Where do we go from here?
Mavro means black, *Aki*, from Crete;
he wears his island like a cross.

III

His gas lamp hisses, filament trembles—
the sound of night escaping.
Salmon-tired tourists move up Hadrianou,
they have made the ocean crossing to come to this:
a street of jewelry shops and plaster,
authentic Greeks in authentic shops.
This city is like a shirt worn inside out.
He waits on the unclaimed corner,
every bag of salted nuts sold is a step
toward home. Nuts, cigarettes, empty canisters of gas—
dark green drip-marks in the paint of his cart.
Green paint, gas lamps, fingerprints of Athens
before the war, before aluminum window frames,
mirrored glass and plastic roll-up shades.
Before orange awnings. Before
        the gods became a circus out of work.

VALPARAISO

Field of zinc—
tin wave stalled
and galvanized against a sky
so summer-blue it flirts
with disaster.

And the houses cry out,
"our bright yellow poverty,
our two eggs served
like the jaundiced eyes
of our poverty;

our beautiful brown children
run flame-like through
the crimson edges of our poverty
and still our song rises
from oily smokestacks."

Valparaiso, Valparaiso
whose stripped tankers
lie like cadavers
under bright lights
in the floating shipyard.

Whose elevators,
patrons of rust,
climb the desolate hills
in the midsummer sun—
faith in rusted cable.

And the shacks bloomed fuchsia,
titanium white
and "candle-wrapper blue"
on the buttressed,
dog-traveled alleys

with boat paint
your sailors lifted
from a drunk captain
sailing unshaven
in a rum-tinted dream.

Valparaiso—
whose shattered length
is a woman staring
from a window
at the unrepentant sea.

A NIGHT IN BELLAVISTA

A glass breaks in Bellavista
and the moon lets the mountain slip
like a skirt around her ankles.
I saw the sky go dark blue as open water
while a plane, thundering over
the airport palms, leans its tail-smoke
across the black wall of the Andes.
The dogs slip past the tables,
ears flat, eyes rolling as they dodge
the drunks and sidewalk waiters.
Something about the night is bigger,
and the women grow more beautiful,
their laughter breaking the darkness,
as it spins from their painted lips.
The Mapocho river churns beneath
a concrete bridge strung with vendors—
the water is the color of mud.
This water eats men, chews lovers,
spits its aggregated memory
into the jaws of the Pacific.
Something about the night is bigger
in the height of summer while your shirt
sticks to your chest and the table
sinks under bottles of beer.
You are vanishing in Santiago
with the wild dogs on broad avenues
by the river that slings its brown effluvium
past the gas lamps and grinning drunks.

ANDRIANA RIZOS

Andriana Rizos is pursuing her MA degree in English and Creative Writing at Hofstra University. She has read her poetry at the Ear Inn, Cosi's Bar, the Bowery Poetry Club, and the Cornelia Street Café. She has also coordinated poetry programs at Uniondale Public Library and Jamaica Day School of Saint Demetrios, where she is a seventh and eighth grade English, Creative Writing, and Social Studies teacher. Andriana's parents came from Thessaly, Greece, which provides a source of inspiration for her writing.

GHAZAL OF AGAPI

Commit theft of mind, take hearts to prevail, Agapi.
It takes solemn tears when indecisive hope is frail: Agapi.

If only you can try and comprehend its reasoning,
escape enslavement to unveil Agapi.

Priority–your heart needs to melt before your tears could flow.
I can't succeed in that for I've watched you fail, Agapi.

Melody–let it be beautiful, add it to your voice.
Breathe mindless confusion, then softly exhale, "Agapi."

Rise up from underneath your prison of restraint.
Though Andriana will perish, one cannot bail–Agapi.

TODAY

You died in me today;
misjudged
and afflicted me

with all the pain you bore
when they lifted your unsoiled hands
and injected your palms with the voids you infest in me,

the way I spread my arms
as a sick child, desperately
longing for the hug never received in my cold bedroom.

It was you who never embraced me,
tormented me to feel
the lashes of your whippings.

I lit a candle today.

Placed my middle finger on my thumb
and pointed to the touch with a touch;
my embrace to you

lifted to my forehead that once sheltered you,
lowered to the chasm of my stomach now struggling to contain you,
carried up to my right shoulder smothered in black fabric,

crossed over to my left,
careless,
unsinistered.

Three times, I did this,
before the fully formed palm of my hand
rested on my weakened stomach,

kissed your icon and turned back
to face the flame I did not blow out.
The flame that did nothing, said nothing.

Now, gone like a child with dreams,
arms lagging down, left again
with no touch and just as many words,

you turned your perfect shoulder.
Still, I lit a candle today
before I extinguished your name.

POPPED STITCH

Everyone wants to be someplace else.
I just want to be someplace.
I'd drive until the ends of nowhere meet
and I'm entangled in its knot.
There, resting on the middle suture
I'd stitch myself whole
so that I might think young again.
I'm here,
shredded.
Entombed
in tragedies taking over the age.
Identities are lost to authorities
stealing the language out of our mouths,
yet we rely on a single knot as protection.
With enough force, entities are severed,
and when the suture has come undone
we are back here rather than someplace.

HELEN RUVELAS

Helen Ruvelas is a first generation Greek-American. She grew up in a household that spoke only Greek and received her only English-language education in the schools she attended. She began writing poetry at the age of 13 and continued in both Greek and English. In September of 2003, she found a nurturing and supportive group in the Poetry Workshop of the Rancho Mirage Public Library in California. During the last three years, the group critiqued, encouraged, and emboldened her to put her energy into her passion for poetry.

FAMILY PORTRAIT

I sit alone
imprisoned by
overstuffed chairs
tree burdened with tinsel
neatly opened boxes

the photograph seizes
the black of a white moment
painful fidelity of
mother father and
chubby-cheeked child

fifty years later
that moment escapes
its box and
I again sit alone
scared to move

from the anthology *The 84th Moon*

YOU HOLD YOURSELF PROUD

the photo
you were young
your face
chiseled

                                                cliffs
                                              ravines
                                            here hold
                                            your love

black waves
flow over
furrowed
brow

                                                rage
                                            contours
                                          your moist
                                                 mouth

black rage
line years
fear draws
your mouth

                                              veils
                                            soothe
                                        your courage
                                            my sorrow

black veils
repentant
of a life
not lived

                                    I hang on that rock

NICHOLAS SAMARAS

Nicholas Samaras won The Yale Series of Younger Poets Award for his first book, *Hands of the Saddlemaker*. A limited-edition book, *Survivors of the Moving Earth*, was published in Europe. Samaras's works (poetry, prose, and translations) have appeared in *The New Yorker, The New York Times, Poetry, Kenyon Review*, and elsewhere—and he has received grants from the National Endowment of the Arts and State Grants from Colorado, New York, and Florida. A 2004 Lilly Endowment Foundation Fellowship sent him to Greece and Germany where he completed a new manuscript of poetry, *SIMKO*, based on the life and death of Svetozar Daniel Simko, the Slovakian poet and translator of German poetry. Also, Samaras is in the process of completing a memoir, *The Lost City of Pekin*, in which he focuses on living underground for eleven years and the psychology of small villages in this world. Samaras comes from the Greek Island of Patmos and lived for several years in Thessaloniki, Greece. He has also lived in England, Austria, Switzerland, Yugoslavia, Jerusalem, and America. Samaras has just completed teaching at the University of South Florida and, as of this writing, he has moved back to New York City, where he is investigating employment.

STUDIO APARTMENT

1. Exile from is also to

A man may count the number of his lives
by how many houses he ever lived in, in how many countries.

My education in England, the way I still spell. My childhood
on the Lido de Jeselo in Italy, in Switzerland, Patmos, Thessaloniki,

and the parishes across America, until I was an only child in Quincy,
Massachusetts, my single father and I living in Apartment 11-M,

the final settlement of our home—until New York years later,
I met you and visited your studio apartment on East 27th Street

in Manhattan, only to discover you lived in Apartment 11-M.
From then, you were my missing brother in the City,

in the bohemian years where I'd drive in from the Island,
two hours each way. Your apartment became my Manhattan,

shuttling between Columbia classes, being trained how to think.
Our humour grew into routines. You taught me how to affect

an inquisitor's East Berlin accent, where we developed the comedy
of secret police. And my standard line: see that parking space

across from your apartment? I parked there once.
Only a New Yorker with a car would get that.

In the noise that became music. In the Columbia, bohemian years,
the time that remains a good time, expatriate lives and homes converged.

2. Exile as Place and Resonance

When does life become lifestyle?
You lived your life in one room.

The studio apartment. Three steps from bed
to bathroom. Ten steps to the closet kitchen.

Square footage crammed and overflowing with your years.
The efficiency, inefficient.

Comrade Simko, everything bespoke exile at home.
The way your name shifted in America. The way

you shuffled from chair to bed, and called yourself
"Dandog." And only the bookshelves permanent.

Daniel, when does lifestyle become a life?
Everything about your place was resonant with the world.

Most nights, Tibet and China steamed on the desk
that was the dining table. Europe sat on the long shelves,

century by decade. The Danube floated in the wine glasses.
Dusty on the floor, the portable television was America.

Compatriots were contemporary volumes, stacked
high in a labyrinth across the wood floor. In every country,

every village and city, then, what did we ever find
but the patchwork of ourselves?

It was all good, Daniel.
If we were no country, we could be every country.

Displaced by the world's history, we inhabited the world.
And you can only find the world through exile.

SEPTEMBER IN THARRI

A late heat pressed the air—and the landscape
of the monastery with its terraced hills
always looked like Chinese etchings.

The brush of pine trees. A scalloped garden.
Ancient slate benches hyphenating the hills.
Framed like that in the brief distance,

a black-robed master was observed
to gesture in emphasis to his student,
breeze swaying the branches above them.

You've returned to this image many times.
It was September. There was heat, wind, a sketched vista.
Which of the three men were you?

THE NEED FOR PRIESTS

I

A white marble table.
Black striations pulsing through the stone.

A goblet of still wine.
Wine so deep in the hollow,
so darkly blooded, it is almost black.
      When we lean to the cup, our eyes stare back.

We are the dark angels.
Shadows at a christening.

II

Knowing only our wooden chairs at work,
the same roads home and the predictable
food on our plates, the placement
of our shoes at the bedside
and the heaviness of blankets melting
us into the forms of our bodies,
we have a terrible need for priests.

We need those black others to go beyond themselves
and bring back the stories, take the effort away.
We want admonishing priests, to expose them for what we really are.
Always we are attacking the better parts of ourselves.
Contemptuous of the kind, we secretly
envy the guiltless evil.
Purity frightens, as much as we desire it.

Because of this, we have priests to love and despise.
We need priests to kill them.
We are a black tapestry
who want our clergy to wear black forever,
to be lost in muslin robes,
to be as apart from us as we are
separate from ourselves.

We have prayers said for us, but we are mute in sleep.
We adore the bones of saints—soft
with centuries, yellow and assiduous.
We need priests to revere.
We kill them to venerate their deaths,
believe we grow pious by this,
waft beeswax candles in the air
while saints ashen underground.
Because we must always be burying or uncovering,
we need the voices of priests, to have
something to bury.
To spend our lives on this.

At best, we insist
on being dragged to salvation.
Distrustful of proximity, we are content
to look out windows,
to feel the panes on our fingertips.

Our ears strain for faraway music,
a chant across borders,
and the muscles in our backs twinge
but there will always be
a country we cannot get to.
      True savoring is in the denial.

This is why
we have the need for priests,
why we remain
with one hand pressed to our throats,
faces turned like flowers to the warmth of light,
peering off,
settled on an icy edge of Paradise.

APPROACH

It begins with leaving.

It begins with leaving to come back to you always.

I will come to you in snow
when the earth grows hard for footsteps

and the white mist wraithlike on water.

I will go, and keep intoning
your name....

I will give names to the nights

and watch the endless stars
in slow revolution,

mark the world
by how the constellations change position.

It begins with leaving.
It must begin.

There is earth, smoke, starlight.
There is turning.

I will come to you in snow.

THE SOUND OF MY VOICE LIKE A FOREIGN LANGUAGE

You sleep broken hours.
You are a voice
heavy with sleep and heavy with waking.

Winter rakes over the land, the fallow fields.
You are chaff.
In long years, you will whiten.

When wind carries in from far countries,
you hear whispering from a wilderness
a voice that sounds vaguely like yours.

Unclench your teeth, your body—
embrace the changing, the *metanoia*,
the terrible, pure light.

Work your way to nothing
until you are nude with freedom.
You will give

your hands away
without thinking
of what will be

returned to you.
You will give your hands
away.

MINAS SAVVAS

Minas Savvas recently retired after teaching at San Diego State University for 38 years. He has widely published poetry, reviews, translations, and articles not only on Greek literature and culture, but also on Shakespeare, Chekhov, Marlowe, and critical theory. For several years, he was one of the chosen nominators for the Nobel Prize in Literature. He is the recipient of several awards, including one from the National Endowment for the Humanities, the Best Reviewer Award from *World Literature Today*, and the Alexandrian Award from California's Hellenic Cultural Society.

For many years, he wrote articles for several Greek-American publications, but his more professional publications have appeared in journals like *The Yale Review, The New York Review of Books*, the *Antioch Review,* and dozens of other prestigious journals. Savvas is also one of the 4-5 translators of the poetry of Yannis Ritsos. He has published four volumes of Ritsos poems in translation—including *Chronicle of Exile, The Subterranean Horses, The House Vacated,* and *Peculiar Gestures.*

Most recently, the Italian journal *Foro Ellenico* published an analytical retrospective of Savvas's poetry, by Tiziana Cavasino.

THE CEMETERY IN KUKUVAUNES

The dead are hidden from the city;
They like being irrelevant, uninvolved.
The slabs of stone do not even glitter
Under the Greek moon. The thyme fills
The air, though there is no wind,
And the grass grows recklessly.

Three olive trees mark the black horizon,
Obscuring the silent distance.
A kite dangled on the olive branch
Hangs like a soul obstructed.

I walk my 37 years back to the car;
The bouzouki singer complains on the radio:
"Every smile is a lie
since you left me ..."
The engine carves the silence ...
Half of my life under the stones.

THE ONLY CERTAINTY
Written at an NEH Conference at U.C. Santa Cruz, for my "special needs" son Peter

The jaybirds squeaked loudest
When structuralism was mentioned,
But I, the scholar, thought I understood.
Then when some spoke of the sestina
I rushed to compose one
Only to make excuses later.

As a tourist in town, I was reminded
By a bloody accident how hard it all can be,
And my ignorance, like an uppercut,
Sent me to the Boardwalk amusements,
To those palliatives for boredom and chance.

There my fatherness surfaces, and you in front
My Peter, thoughts as private as blood:
Those numbers that obsess you,
Those phrases you so often repeat,
The thermometer's three digits
When your fevered eyes glistened . . .

Now, I am patting a boy on the head
And he thinks it's for him,
I toss away half of my ice cream cone
And my colleague thinks I don't like it,
I wipe my eyes at the restaurant
And the waiter does not know it's love.

WOMEN AT FIFTY

Women at fifty wear their bodies
like the fragile warmth of autumn,
their crescents of pleasure are moons
that slice our darkness with splendor.

In them, something more giving
replaces that exquisite resistance of flesh.
Their "yes" is like a juicy pear in the mouth,
a defiant response to mortality's terror.

Women at fifty know the script in a lover's eyes,
they know of fleeting things like a sigh or a touch,
of the dexterity in a lover's tongue,
of the words that can thrill and betray.

Women at fifty know of the skull
under the lover's kiss, they seize passion
as if it will soon vanish; they are
warriors in our strife with time.

Now, take Della before that tactless mirror
yielding to gravity as to her lover's arms:
soon the lines that web into a fuller bloom
will lead to a place where beauty outwears its need.

Della at fifty, like others who know,
goes to bed thinking of the center of things,
of the vanity of seasons and games,
of the silence at the end of rage or confusion.

Her alpenglow eyes rehearse the fading of all light.
She dreams of the child she'll never have.

HILARY SIDERIS

Hilary Sideris grew up in a small town in northern Indiana. She attended Indiana University and The Writers' Workshop at The University of Iowa. Her poems have appeared in *Barrow Street, Good Foot, Green Mountains Review, Gulf Coast, Mid-American Review, Iris, Salamander,* and *Women's Studies Quarterly.* As far as she knows, she is not related to David Sedaris.

DOUG CRAIG

What did he mean he *saw her*?

Cigarette behind his ear.

Checking his hair in my reflector shades.

Talker, bluffer, gruffer than my father.

Held me down, hand over my mouth.

The neighbors stopped complaining.

Clucked their tongues in earshot.

Nights he shoved me into traffic.

Days I called the cops, hung up.

from *Barrow Street*

ROUTE SEVEN RIVERLAWN ADDITION

Home base of horseplay
zoned for tornadoes,
box on a lot, abode

of wall-to-wall gold shag
& tag turned tackle,
liar, pants on fire,
torque & tongue.

We dwelled ranch style
at the level of gravel, knelt
& excelled at groveling:

down the faux oak paneled hall,
one door that locked,
his scissors cocked
to coax it open.

SEX

I confess I like
mine from a can,

product of Greece,
Portugal, Spain,

odor & shimmer
when I lock my office,

pull the E-Z open
tab & spatter

calendar,
curriculum!

GEOMETRY

How can you be the you who called
the table of contents *the plate
of compliments*, who named the water
bottle *baba wayo?* Tonight we cram

isosceles, scalene & how a rhombus
differs from a square. I love your
getting-wavy hair, the way your lashes
graze the page, their half-moon curve,

like your father's, when you nod off.
I don't know which I prefer: math
from your mouth or your textbook's
definition of a line, the part where

it goes on in both directions forever.

from *Four Corners*

ELENI SIKELIANOS

Eleni Sikelianos is the author of one book of nonfiction and five books of poetry. Most recent titles are *The California Poem* (Coffee House Press) and *The Book of Jon* (City Lights). Her poems have been translated into French, Spanish, Catalan, Arabic, Romanian, Croation, Slovenian, and Serbian. Among the numerous awards she has received for her poetry, nonfiction, and translations are a National Endowment for the Arts Award, a Fulbright Arts Fellowship, The National Poetry Series, a Seeger Fellowship at Princeton University, and a New York Foundation for the Arts Award. Sikelianos received her MFA in 1991 from what was then The Naropa Institute, where she studied with many of the most exuberant and influential living poets of our times. She currently lives in Colorado with the novelist Laird Hunt and their daughter Eva Grace; she teaches in the Creative Writing Program at the University of Denver.

FIRST GREEK POEM

I the roses love in the garden of Adonis
I the salted fry of marguerite love, the one chamomile, the tiny white
       that snaps dancing in the gutter with funny
I reddest poppy painted in blood love
Love I the final columned crown
Ever a flower inventory wept, I dreamt
Of death, wedding flower; treading
       purple will I go
Into that drowning house
With wet little lambs one-day old (*arnakia*), white horses (*waves*)
       lapping at the heart-knobs
When the slave pumped the handle, and the water rose

from *The Monster Lives of Boys & Girls*, copyright © 2003 by Eleni Sikelianos. Reprinted with the permission of Green Integer Books, www.greeninteger.com.

FOOTNOTE TO THE LAMBS

1. You shall hope to know the power of the imagination
2. You shall wish to be intellectual, be somebody; you shall
     forget about bombs
3. You shall dream of a caravan circling lush trees
     & live in dirt balls, with no sugar, no swaying allowed
4. You, loveliness in your Grecian tires, good citizens
     of sheepdom, smoking hashish, hush
5. You shall come from the Azure

from *The Monster Lives of Boys & Girls*, copyright © 2003 by Eleni Sikelianos. Reprinted with the permission of Green Integer Books, www.greeninteger.com.

IKARIA'S TIDEPOOLS

the water's surface talks back to waves in scaly
(windswept) shapes, & the sea shows us
micro monsters caught
in writhing waves, aspiring
to wrest themselves free
of rock
bottom
shore or
sea

(I dream it
as if I were the sea, adamant, sea's
big muscle
squeezing me)

nudibranch or sea-
millipede dressed to match
the evening sun, every
leg (shape
of a question mark) shuffling
sea

ghost shrimp
pounds on a gastropod's trap
door, spiny fish nibble toes, crab

eats crab, some scrap of purple
flesh flutters in currents; here
as in every tide pool, a minute-by-minute it-
could-be-curtains

knots up around us—
Akilah's son, Judy's sister,
my father; soldiers and civilians
tonight; tonight
the net will tighten

around some-
one;   Let it
not be me
or someone
I love, let it
not be any
animal
rock
or sea   Let it
flow on
between itself
life : death : life : death

from *The California Poem*, copyright © 2004 by Eleni Sikelianos. Reprinted with the permission of Coffee House Press, www.coffeehousepress.org.

DIANA STAMATELATOS-THEOCHARIS

Diana Stamatelatos-Theocharis is a Greek-American woman, born and raised in New York City by Greek immigrants from the island of Kefalonia. She descends from a long line of poets in both the oral and written traditions, including her grandfathers Dionisios Georgopoulos and Dionisios "Tzitzikas" Stamatelatos. When she is not writing, she is painting, singing, acting, or taking photographs. To her, all of these are an extension of one another. Without them, she is missing her voice.

She holds a BA in Theatre Arts & a BS in English Literature from Queens College, the City University of New York. She has been previously published in *Mondo Greco* and has read at various poetry readings.

She shares her life with her husband George and their cat Espresso.

FOR YIAYIA & PAPOU

       sometimes i drive through flushing cemetery
    with a cup of coffee to share with you.
      i sit in my car
with the windows rolled down
   to hear the breeze carry
       your voices into my ears
         once again.

FOR FEDERICO GARCIA LORCA, "HE DIED AT DAWN"

night of no stars
no trace of a moon
cloudless running water.
i look for the tracks
of your kisses, as you once
tenderly placed them on my body
like birthmarks, i count them.
each of the many times you loved me
in passion
where i got lost and wanted
to die without you.
you found me and sacrificed my
heart to the moon
as its cold hands touched
my hot flesh; they burned
and now i have two prints
on my pale breasts
and they long to be suckled
by your children.

SMOKING REALITY THROUGH CUBAN CIGARS IN KEY WEST

fruit basket
sitting on a kitchen counter
in front of me
filled with the fruits
of my insides.

i have a pen in my hand
that makes round circles.
perfection.
imperfect perfection.
circle closes
and goes round and round
like the pretty white
horse with the gold and leather
reins i used to ride
at flushing meadow park.

i wanted to be the lone ranger.
i wanted to be the wild bill.
i thought i could be calamity jane
shooting wild and dressing like a man.

a strong woman.

my garden is weeded
with make a wish
blowing flowers. little girls
run through hemingway's
garden. palm trees
now have christmas lights
and giant snowflakes.
does santa come here too?

giant plantation houses
next to white trash trailer homes;
lovely distorted realities and banana leaves.

i don't want to be the princess in a fairytale.
i don't want to need to be saved.

TRYFON TOLIDES

Tryfon Tolides was born in Korifi Voiou, Greece. He moved to the United States at age six and grew up around, and worked in, his father's pizza place. He has completed a BFA in Creative Writing at the University of Maine, and an MFA at Syracuse University. He has received a Reynolds Scholarship, the 2004 Foley Poetry Prize, and his manuscript, *An Almost Pure Empty Walking*, a 2005 National Poetry Series selection, was published by Penguin in July 2006. His work has appeared in *America*, *Atlanta Review*, *Mondo Greco*, *Poetry Daily*, *Worcester Review*, and elsewhere. He lives in Farmington, Connecticut.

ADDRESS

Late August in the South where summers go on.
Hummingbird and red hyacinth. Breeze and lizards

and banana leaves. Violet bougainvillea
gently twisting in the hanging pots.

Ceramic fixtures on telephone poles. Black wires
arched across the pastel blue sky, in the sun's

harsh creamy heat. Sway, and keep swaying, Things.

I TOLD MYSELF

You need to record this.
You need to say:
tonight I went for a walk.
The sky was lit up
a deep radiating blue.
Something made me skip
and trot and turn
all the way around
while walking
and put out my arms
to make an airplane
and lean the wings and
my body to make turns
and be joyed and be joined
with the sky
as if it were my friend
or my dead mother.
I stopped and touched
the living density of trees.
I lifted my nose to pink oleander
and then sprang again
as if the earth were a kind of sky
and walking, an almost unwilled
floating, as if I were
one of the miraculous birds
or a walking tree.

NEW MOON

There were two sparrows
in the quince tree this morning.
I saw them. The roosters
crowed then and again
at three or four after my siesta.
When I went out tonight
to walk, a song came to me
and I stopped. It said itself
through me two or three times
using my voice and my entire self.
I had nothing to write it down with
and I didn't want to go back
into the house for pencil and paper.
I walked on and forgot what that was.

POEM WRITTEN STANDING AND LOOKING OUT THE WINDOW

Something blossoming
outside, white buds
off a tree. What's that
truck tire doing discarded
in the yard? And the pile
of plywood? Another
tree, leafless, gray downcast
branches, today's rain
and wind, and true spring
cold. I've twisted open
the blinds. I remember
delivering liquor to Nick,
rich, finished with work.
He'd answer the door
in a bath robe. Strings swelling,
or tempered elevator music
of desolate love. Vic
Damone or Dean Martin
driving the alcohol deeper
into the walls and furniture
and carpet. The curtains always
drawn shut, often in bright
summer weather. You could not
see the shadows of light
in the window corners.

DENO TRAKAS

Deno Trakas is Professor of English and Director of the Writing Center at Wofford College in Spartanburg, South Carolina. He's published fiction and poetry in magazines such as *The Denver Quarterly* and *Oxford American* and two chapbooks of poetry, the most recent of which is *human & puny*, which includes 20 monochrome watercolors by his sister Irene. He's won five South Carolina Fiction Project Prizes and a South Carolina Individual Artist Grant. He's working on two novels and a book about Greek immigrants in South Carolina and is always looking for people with interesting stories to tell.

END OF AUGUST 2005
for MD

Under a smudged and sticky sun
they lounge in chaise,
in bathing suits and shades
with rum and Cokes in plastic cups
on the deck of their new old house.

They're young, poor, and happy,
their dreams as loud and brassy
as trumpets playing the French Quarter
where they love to go, a bus ride
from their blighted neighborhood.

Their dreams rise like moons
above their cluttered view,
above the sunken city, the shrinking wetlands,
the oily Gulf where a spindly hurricane
waves at south Florida and turns north.

Their dreams are as big and easy
as their house is cramped and messy—
but it has a proud new roof
so tight that when the water raises
them into the trusses

of the axeless attic, with floating
boxes of Christmas decorations
and winter clothes, the bridge
of the nose touches the beam of the ridge,
the solid levee of the body, the breach of the soul.

THE SMALLER HOUSE

> *"All that happens when I get something wonderful like this award is that my neuroses move into a larger house."*
> —*Akhil Sharma*

We've moved into a smaller house,
mother, father, daughter, son and dog,
far from convenience but close
to claustrophobia, a "fixer upper,"
a fixated dump whose sewer line clogs.

In the masterless bedroom, too small
for a king, my wife hammers
nails like migraines into the wall,
then hangs our children on hooks,
and when the phone screams, shivers.

Her mother wants to see our little nook,
she'll bring a plant, she'll help us clean
and Martha Stewart our squalor—she'll even cook.
My daughter, sentenced to unpacking dishes,
squashes roaches to Rage Against the Machine.

My son flings his things and sonofabitches
his sorryass father, downsized again.
He hurls his own hard rock and wishes
he could split this crib, this shitshack,
this hell where death begins.

On my belly I slither the pitchblack
crawlspace to find the furnace and light the pilot—
insects skitter and spider webs claw my back—
but I'm desperate for one small success
below these joists of dry rot.

I bump and fumble and finally gain access
to the inner switches, light a match—
the saving flame catches, the furnace groans
like a testy god. Outside the dog scratches
the patch of grass, trying to find a bone.

from *human & puny*, and *A Millennial Sampler of South Carolina Poetry*

ALL GOD'S MAIL

comes to me here
at the post office in Old Jerusalem.
I read what I can, English and Hebrew, though it costs me
money and faith, faith in a God who answers prayers.

One old man, poor and pure, begged for 5000 shekels
for medical help for his daughter. Moved, we collected
4300 and sent it. He wrote back, "Thank you God, but next time
don't send money through the mail—those guys stole 700."

Usually, of course, I don't answer—how could I?
What would God's rejection say? "God is closed"
or "God is unable to fulfill your request at this time."
Even worse to give false hope.

So I take the letters—from a pregnant Christian girl,
a Muslim mother with AIDS, a bereft Jewish father—
to the Wailing Wall, the western wall of the Temple Mount,
where, by legend, God's presence is steadfast and eternal.

I cram them in the cracks between the massive stones
which, within reach, are polished by the touch of human hands
beseeching God, hoping for Holy molecules or miracles
for their own fingers or for those they love.

Today, among the hundreds, an Israeli soldier stands beside me,
head down, Uzi shouldered, right hand on the wall, and prays
for his buddy, killed by a sniper, to find peace, happiness,
and sex too, why not, in heaven, then backs away

and bumps into a tourist taking his picture.
But the letters in my hands ask for so much more,

a marvelous abundance of grief and need,
evidence of an inept God, a vengeful God,

or a God who's walked away from this Holy
place, where men fight wars to pray.
I deliver God's letters to the wall where
they will be answered by God's weather.

from *Kakalak: An Anthology of Carolina Poets*

LABOR DAY, PEN AND SPADE
for SH

I dig too, hand and arm,
but in a smaller, private yard.
Last summer's droughted grass
has come back weedy lush.

An expert once explained to me
there's no such thing as a weed,
only a plant in the wrong place,
and here there should be grass.

So I yank up plants misplaced.
Usually I manage to clear the surface,
sometimes I even get roots
and depth, usually not.

I'd like to think I have a skill,
my fingers managing the soil,
weeding, planting, spreading lime
and fertilizer with precise timing,

but mine is a fallible instinct
and no one who's expert thinks
my meager work is worth advice,
so I'm left to learn my own devices.

My judgment is unsettled—
some of the weeds are pretty
with clusters of purple flowers,
and I'd like to make allowance.

But I go with what I see around,
trim, level, uniform lawns—
I pull the weeds efficiently,
the purple flowers snap off easily.

from *In the West of Ireland*; also *45/96: A Ninety-Six Sampler of South Carolina Poetry*

GRANDFATHER

Did you know, Papou, that you alone
cross me with faith? Your cigar
is the only smell from death, your stubble face
the only friction at my edge of knowing.

I can be so adamant in doubt,
but your psalter chant, still Greek
in memory, passes, solemn,
to my altar boy ear—the ritual we shared—

and the sight of you, so white in the stains
of religion, is more believable
than any icon, any priest
(you were real, a Yankee fan).

I believed in you and you believed.
Now, as I grow through changing types of war,
the kneeling peace of then makes no sense,
but I know, with all senses,
the memory of you, the presence of you.

from the Joseph Nichols Poster Poem Series

*Literary and Poetry Books
from Somerset Hall Press:*

Fate and Ambiguity in Oedipus the King, by Stelios Ramfos, translated by Norman Russell. A literary and philosophical reflection on the world-famous play, with a Foreword by renowned actor Olympia Dukakis.

Golden Anthology: Writings of a Greek-American Soldier in Korea, edited by Dean Papademetriou. Poems and stories by a Greek immigrant who was killed while heroically serving in the United States Army in Korea.

Islands, by Robert Zaller. Poems inspired by the Greek islands.

Pomegranate Seeds: An Anthology of Greek-American Poetry, edited by Dean Kostos.

Sister of Darkness: A Memoir, by Lili Bita. The powerful story of a woman's journey of self-discovery and personal liberation.

Stations of the Sun, by Roger Finch. Poems inspired by life and travels in Asia.

Thirty Years in the Rain: The Selected Poetry of Nikiforos Vrettakos, translated by Lili Bita and Robert Zaller. Poems by one of the most celebrated twentieth-century Greek poets.

For more information about these books, including how to order them, please visit www.somersethallpress.com.

www.ingramcontent.com/pod-product-compliance
Ingram Content Group UK Ltd.
Pitfield, Milton Keynes, MK11 3LW, UK
UKHW041431180426

11947UKWH00007B/390